Young Lorenzo

EARLY LIFE
OF D. H. LAWRENCE

EMILY, GEORGE, ERNEST, ADA, Mrs. LAWRENCE,
DAVID HERBERT and Mr. LAWRENCE.

Figures left to right reading from top.

Young Lorenzo

EARLY LIFE
OF D. H. LAWRENCE

*CONTAINING HITHERTO
UNPUBLISHED LETTERS, ARTICLES
AND REPRODUCTIONS OF PICTURES*

BY

ADA LAWRENCE
AND
G. STUART GELDER

NEW YORK / RUSSELL & RUSSELL

1966

FIRST PUBLISHED IN 1931
REISSUED, 1966, BY RUSSELL & RUSSELL
A DIVISION OF ATHENEUM HOUSE, INC.
L.C. CATALOG CARD NO: 66—11880

PRINTED IN THE UNITED STATES OF AMERICA

CONTENTS

LIST OF ILLUSTRATIONS

XI

YOUNG LORENZO

On 27 December, 1875, John Arthur Lawrence, a mining contractor, and Lydia Beardsall were married in Sneinton Church, Nottingham. After living for a short time at Sutton in Ashfield and Old Radford they went to Eastwood, and he continued to work at Brinsley Colliery where he had been employed since he was seven years of age. They had five children — George Arthur, William Ernest, Emily, David Herbert, and Lettice Ada. Last year David Herbert died in France. To some he was a writer of obscene books and a painter of obscene pictures. To others he was a genius and one of the most significant artists of his generation. In some respects he was to them the most significant. His work was an outrage upon the conventional moral standards which in his eyes were as dangerous as they were useless. The post-war age was never to him what it still seems to be to our newspaper writers — an age of intellectual and moral freedom in which progress is allowed to march as quickly as she likes in every sphere of life. He was no reformer, excepting inasmuch as he inspired others to discard prejudices and try to see life as clearly as he tried to see it. He was ashamed of nothing excepting lies and the evil they breed. He wrote as simply about sexual functions as about coal mines and table-spoons because they are all a part of everyday life, and he could see

4

no reason why one should not mention things with which everyone is perfectly well acquainted.

But because sex is something which everyone possesses, but about which we are all supposed to know nothing outside conjugal bedrooms, Lawrence is attacked as a betrayer of the young and a polluter of our moral water-supply. He mentioned the unmentionable, and because of that one would imagine upon reading reviews and newspaper articles about his work that he never mentioned anything else.

Apparently his enemies have not read his Nottinghamshire novels, or perhaps they do not contain the matter which provides sensational headlines. What Thomas Hardy is to Wessex, and Mary Webb to Shropshire, he is to Nottinghamshire. He did not bother to invent much fact. He wrote about actual places and actual people, some of whom are still living in the same places. His writing about this coal-blasted countryside was the beginning of his reaction to ugliness which became unbearable to him so that it made him physically ill to live amongst it. He did not compromise. He never pretended that there was something artistically picturesque about the rotting roof of a miner's home. He did not bother about political arguments. He saw that some of the most lovely country in England had been insanely turned into an industrial midden, and that thousands of men and women had been thrown on to it to scratch for a beggarly existence. Like Jesus Christ and St. Francis of Assisi, he embarrassed people by telling the truth whenever he spoke about anything.

It has been noticed that whenever men have embarrassed their worldly peers too much by telling the truth, their worldly peers have made efforts to remove them from the attention of the public. In the old days they executed them or threw them into dungeons. Nowadays they pillory them in the press and police-court, and tell lies about them. This is done so effectively that even intelligent people are deceived and believe that Lawrence is that mythical invention of muck-raking journalism — a sex novelist. Many have been surprised and disappointed not to find any of the qualities attributed to him by Grub Street liars. That is the irony of the

7

history of the artist. His name has filled the columns of the press. He has been mentioned wherever a newspaper is sold, yet few know him. They know nothing of his youth and the influences which drove him to write and paint the things he did. They know that some pictures of nude people were seized by the police at an exhibition held in London just before he died, and that a book called " Lady Chatterley's Lover " was burnt by order of the law. But there is so much more to know. It has even been suggested that he began to paint towards the end of his life because paint was a better pornographic medium than ink. They do not know that he began to paint before he began to write articles and novels — studies of flowers and copies of M. Greiffenhagen — and

THE HOUSE IN VICTORIA STREET, EASTWOOD, WHERE D. H. LAWRENCE WAS BORN.

that this " polluter of the young " was a very successful schoolmaster and was congratulated on the manner in which he taught. They know only what they have been told, and most of it is wrong.

Lawrence was born in Victoria Street, Eastwood, on 11 Sept. 1885. There were already three children in the family — George Arthur, William Ernest, and Emily. His father was a handsome, well-built man who before his marriage sang in the church choir and was reputed to be the best dancer in the district. He was a stranger to any but newspaper literature. The mother was of a different breed. Her father had worked as an engineer in the Sheerness dockyard, and she became a school teacher. She read a good deal and wrote poetry.

In "Sons and Lovers" Lawrence tells how Mrs. Morel left Sheerness when she was twenty and met a young fellow named John Field. They fell in love. He became a teacher and went to Norwood. Two years later she heard that he had married his landlady — a widow with property. When she was twenty-three she met Morel who was.

"....well set up, erect, and very smart. He had wavy black hair that shone again, and a vigorous black beard that had never been shaved. His cheeks were ruddy, and his red, moist mouth was noticeable because he laughed so often and so heartily. He had that rare thing, a rich, ringing laugh. Gertrude Coppard had watched him, fascinated. He was so full of colour and animation, his voice ran so easily into comic grotesque, he was so ready and so pleasant

10

with everybody. Her own father had a rich fund of humour, but it was satiric. This man's was different: soft, non-intellectual, warm, a kind of gambolling. She herself was opposite. She had a curious, receptive mind, which found much pleasure and amusement in listening to other folk. She was clever in leading folk on to talk. She loved ideas, and was considered very intellectual. What she liked most of all was an argument on religion, or philosophy or politics with some educated man. This she did not often enjoy.... She was to the miner that thing of mystery and fascination, a " lady ".

A year later they were married. Morel was John Arthur Lawrence. Gertrude Coppard was Lydia Beardsall.

To him his marriage meant one change
— a charming young wife. To her it meant
more than she had dreamed. She had yet
to know Lawrence the miner, and the
mining country. She never became fully
reconciled to either. The change was too
violent. She did not recover from the first
shock of realising that her life would be
one of almost ceaseless monotony among
endless ugliness and dirt. She escaped into
herself and when the children came, lived
alone with them. He was a stranger in the
house.

Arthur Lawrence was a butty. A butty is
a man in charge of a stall * at the coal-face.
Three or four men work under his direction

---

* A section of the coal face.

and he pays them their wages from the money he receives from the owner for the coal hewn. He sometimes received good money. When he had a stall which yielded coal grudgingly his share decreased. His wife kept a small shop for a time, whether because she needed more money than he gave her or because she wanted something to occupy her mind, her children do not remember, but Mrs Lawrence sold lace caps and aprons and linen, etc., in the front room of the house. There was no tram or bus route to Nottingham, and when the miners visited the city they went either by rail or in the parcel carrier's van. They more frequently walked. Eastwood consisted of a drab main street and hundreds of niggardly houses. The largest store was in the market-place, and belonged to George

Cullen — John Houghton of " The Lost
Girl " — who had a passion for beautiful
clothes, and filled his windows with them
to the amusement of the mining folk, to
whom he was eventually compelled to sell
them at ridiculously low prices.

Besides Brinsley, there were five other
pits in the neighbourhood, Moor Green,
Underwood, High Park, Watnall and
King's. Their ugly heads still rear out of
what might have been some of the loveliest
country in England, a country of long hills
and deep valleys, now begrimed with smoke
and littered with the garbage of heavy
industry. The trees that remain are dying,
their trunks choked with tarry muck from
the great chimneys. When Arthur Lawrence
was a lad, Squire Walker, the pit owner,

14

combined gentlemanly pleasures with coal-getting. He was a patron of cricket and horse-racing. He was still a countryman, despite the pits on the other side of his fence. The estates of the gentry stood magnificently aloof from the backyard ashpit atmosphere of the miners' houses. Now they are being swallowed up by speculative housebuilders, and their owners are fleeing to more secluded places. The mines have gone too deep and too far. They are undermining the things for which they were first sunk.

When Lydia Beardsall and John Lawrence first went to live at Eastwood it was considered disgraceful for a woman to be seen in a public house. Many women were lonely. Mrs. Lawrence was perhaps the

15

most lonely of all for she had nothing to say to her neighbours and they had nothing to say to her. They had nothing in common. She would have been lonely if it had been considered the height of propriety for a wife to accompany her husband to the pub. She hated strong drink. She began to attend the Congregational Chapel, and was visited by the minister, with whom she loved to talk. With the birth of each child her life became more burdensome. She had no help.

When David Herbert was about two years old the family left Victoria Street and went to live in the Breach — the " Bottoms " of " Sons and Lovers ". The history of the Lawrence family, as far as D. H. and his sister Ada knew it, begins here.

16

THE HOUSE IN THE BREACH. (The Bottoms of " Sons and Lovers ").

Ada, who was the only constant friend Lawrence ever had until he met his wife, has written of these days:

" I remember nothing of the house where my brother and I were born, for we left when I was only a few months old and Bert was about two years. The Breach consisted of blocks of houses belonging to Barber Walker and Co., the pit-owners. Our house was at the end of a row, with a garden on three sides. I remember so well the white currant bushes by the house and the old fashioned white rose trees in the little front garden. My mother never liked being there, partly because the houses were in a hollow, principally because the backs looked out on to drab patches of garden with ashpits at the bottom.

" So about five years later we moved again, to Walker Street, where a row of six bay-windowed houses had just been built. We loved living here. We had a wonderful view of Brinsley, Underwood, Moorgreen, and the High Park woods in the distance. Immediately in front were the fields which stretched to the Breach-fields which made the best playground one could have. What fun we had round the ancient ash tree which stood just opposite the house — although the moaning wind through its branches scared us as we lay in bed in the winter.

" How nice we thought that Walker Street house, with its comfortable kitchen which always looked so homelike. I close my eyes and see again father's wooden armchair on one side of the fireplace, and mother's little rocking-chair on the other; the sofa, with its shake-up bed covered with pretty red chintz and cushions to match, the little painted dresser, and the book-case with its rows of books of which we were so proud.

" The few pictures we possessed consisted chiefly of quite decorative oleographs, and the high mantelpiece was in keeping with the brass candlesticks and father's black carved iron tobacco jar, side by side with Bert's * inkstand shaped like a gnome sitting on a log.

" We were proud of our front room or parlour with its well made mahogany and

---

* D. H. Lawrence was always known to his family and friends as " Bert ".

horse-hair suite of furniture — the little mahogany chiffonier and the oval Spanish mahogany table, which my mother insisted on covering with a fawn and green tapestry table-cloth to match the Brussels carpet. Here again were oleographs, heavily framed in gilt, and the family portrait in the place of honour over the mantelpiece.

" Although so unpretentious, there was something about our house which made it different from those of our neighbours. Perhaps this was because Mother would have nothing cheap or tawdry, preferring bareness.

" I marvel now at the housework she could do, and the wonderful way in which she managed on the little money my father

20

gave her.   No wonder we all idolised her.
She was small and slight in figure, her brown
hair, sprinkled with grey, brushed straight
back from a broad brow; clear blue eyes
that always looked fearless and unfaltering,
and a delicately shaped nose, not quite
straight owing to an accident which occurred
when she was a girl; tiny hands and feet,
and a sure carriage.   Some people were
ill-natured enough to say that she " put it
on " when she spoke, for her English was
good and her accent so different from that
of the folk round about.

" Try as she might, she could never speak
the local dialect, and we children were
careful about it when we were with her,
even though we let fling among our friends.
She loved to read, and every week piles of
books were fetched from the local library

to be enjoyed when we were all in bed. The minister liked to visit her, and they discussed religion and philosophy, for she was an excellent talker, and had a dry, whimsical, fascinating sense of humour. She was never effusive or demonstrative in any way, yet we felt in her a wealth of love and a security past all understanding.

" At heart she was deeply religious and a stickler for truth, having great contempt for anything petty, vain or frivolous.

" I don't remember seeing her dressed in anything but black and white, or grey, and she never possessed any jewellery. When I was older I persuaded her to have a bodice of mauve, covered with black lace, but she had grave misgivings every time she put it on. How ladylike we thought she looked when dressed for chapel in her black costume and black silk blouse, little black bonnet decorated with black and white ospreys (she never wore a hat), and an elegant black and white feather boa round her neck.

"Before my brother Ernest died we used to listen for her sweet voice singing hymns. After his death I don't remember her singing again.

"We used to wonder that mother and father, so utterly unsuitable to each other, should be married. But when I look back I can remember my father as a handsome man of medium height with black wavy hair, dark brown beard and moustache. He boasted that a razor had never touched his face. He had dark flashing eyes and a ruddy complexion. His voice was very melodious, and for some years he was in the choir at Brinsley church. My mother, who had never visited a mining village, met him at a party in Nottingham, and was attracted by his graceful dancing, his musical voice, his gallant manner and his overflowing humour and good spirits. He, on his side was drawn to the rather quiet, reserved and ladylike girl. Before many months had passed they were married, my mother looking, in the words of her sister, " like an angel " in her dove-coloured silk dress and bonnet. Her brown ringlets were not fastened up until after the birth of her first child.

" I wonder if there would have been quite so much misery in our childhood if mother had been just a little more tolerant. Having been brought up in a strict and Puritanical atmosphere, she was a staunch teetotaller, and would have no strong drink in the house. My father, who had received little education, being sent to work when he was seven, felt no desire to read anything but newspapers. Having little in common with mother, he soon began to seek the more congenial society of his friends in the public house, not solely for the sake of drink, but because in their company he was more sure of himself, and their interests were his interests.

" Mother would wait up for him, at night, her rage seething, until on his arrival it boiled over in a torrent of biting truths which turned him from his slightly fuddled and pleasantly apologetic mood into a brutal and coarse beast. With palpitating hearts we waited until he came to bed, knowing that not until then could we safely sleep.

" He was very clever at his job and handy in the house. When we were all very young he mended our boots and shoes, and was never more happy than when seated tailor-wise on the rug, with the hobbing iron, hammering away and singing at the top of his voice. If the pans and kettles leaked he could always mend them, and when the eight-day clock was out of order we loved to watch him take it to pieces, carefully putting the screws and spare parts in saucers, and boiling the works in a big saucepan to clean them thoroughly.

" As we grew older we shut him more and more out of our lives, and instinctively turned more to mother, and he, realising this, became more and more distasteful in his habits. He was never really intolerable, and if, instead of wanting the impossible from him, we had tried to interest ourselves in the things for which he really cared, we should have been spared many unhappy and sordid scenes.

He was so proud of us all, and after Mother's death when he was asked why he did not marry again he said, " I've had one good woman - the finest woman in the world, and I don't want another ". My brother's description of him in " Sons and Lovers ", when mother was dying, seems to me to be writing too deep for tears. He shows a lost man, bewildered by the realisation that she was going from him, and that somehow he had no part in anything.

My elder brother George, though shorter than the rest of us, was the most handsome member of the family. He had regular features and dark brown wavy hair. He was apprenticed to the picture framing trade with an uncle in Nottingham when Bert and I were quite young, and later became a textile engineer.

Ernest — William of " Son and Lovers " — was born two years after George. Tall, well built, with thick brown hair with reddish tints and twinkling blue eyes, he was the pride of my mother's heart and our ideal of a fine gentleman. He was exceptionally bright at school, and was held up as a pattern to Bert in later years. After leaving school he became a clerk in the Shipley colliery offices, and later worked in the Co-operative Society's office at Langley

Mill. He attended night classes during the winter, and learnt typewriting and shorthand in his spare time. He had keen business instinct, and when he was 21 obtained a responsible position as a clerk in some London shipping offices. He took correspondence lessons in French and German because they were necessary for his work, and he quickly became well acquainted with both languages. His death from pneumonia at the age of 23 cut short what promised to be a brilliant career. Always full of fun and humour, he was the life and soul of the house, and no party seemed complete unless he was there to play the fool. He had a nickname for each of us.

My sister Emily, because of the colour of her hair, was "Injun Top-knot"; Bert whose hair was light brown in

those days was " Billy White-nob "; and I
" Corkscrews ", because of my curls.

Sometimes letters came addressed to
" Billy the White-nob ", 3, Walker St. etc.
We always knew by the postman's face when
there was anything from Ern'. Sometimes
he drew a sketch illustrating some piece of
news and sent it to us.

When our two pet rabbits were
accidentally suffocated in their hutch, Bert
and I decided to bury them properly. He
blacked a shoe box in which we placed the
bodies while I made little wreaths of daisies
and buttercups to place on top. When we
were ready to carry the coffin to a small
grave at the bottom of the garden, Ernest
suddenly appeared wearing a black silk hat

and long black streamers, and carrying one of father's huge white handkerchiefs into which he bellowed so loud and long that the neighbours hurried out to see what was to do. In spite of our real grief at our loss, we collapsed in laughter at the ridiculous faces he was pulling.

Besides being a fine swimmer (I have still some of his prizes), he could jump a great height, and when he came across fences or gates he cleared them with ease, to our pride and joy.

For a short time he worked at Coventry, and came home on his bicycle every week-end. He was proud to tell Mother that some of the fellows swore that he padded his calves, they were so well shaped.

31

When he went to London his homecomings were the greatest events of our lives, and we young children asked for nothing better than to walk down Eastwood Main Street with him, wearing his frock coat and silk hat. The feathers in Mother's bonnet seemed to nod triumphantly.

He became engaged, and then some of his boyishness disappeared. During his last visit home a week or two before his death we noticed how much thinner he was, and how tired. When he was attacked by pneumonia his overworked body was unable to resist it, and mother arrived in London a few hours before he died. He did not recognise her.

Emily was two years younger than Ernest — a wild harum-scarum when very young, but sedate when she reached her teens.

Bert and I loved her to read aloud to us when mother was out. She knitted well, and during each winter made woollen gloves and stockings, working furiously while she thrilled us with adventure stories, such as " Coral Island ", " Swiss Family Robinson " or tales from " Little Folks ".

She was about three-and-a-half when Bert was born, and always helped to mother him, while he in his turn looked after me.

We children played " Lurky " and " Here Come Three Men From Lincolnshire ". Bert usually preferred the company of girls. He detested football and cricket, and I don't remember him taking part in them. But he had a genius for inventing games, especially indoors. On Monday nights, when Mother attended the Women's Guild of which she

33

was secretary, and on Friday — market night — we had the house to ourselves, and ransacked the place to our hearts' content.

We loved to make toffee, and had a little pink mug into which we put sugar, a scrap of butter, and a drop of vinegar, cooking the mixture in the oven. We never gave it time to cook properly. We were afraid that Mother might return early, but the sugary, sticky mess was our ideal of what toffee should be.

Bert was a remarkably fine cook when he grew up. He began his crude experiments when he was a child. One night he decided that we should make potato-cakes. Two friends, Mabel and Emmie, were with us, and we cooked the potatoes, while Bert, arrayed in mother's blue checked apron, worked at the flour with the rolling-pin. We looked on, admiring the deft way in which he patted the mess into little cakes. They certainly smelt nice in the oven, and we could hardly wait for him to cut them. But instead of crisp, savoury morsels we were handed what looked like bits of india rubber which stuck to our teeth and stretched like elastic. Bert tasted his, and in a doubtful voice he said, " It's nice, isn't it? " " Yes ", we said, hesitatingly, not daring to differ, for he was the head of all our games. For a few moments we nibbled, anxiously watching his face and trying hard not to shudder at each bit swallowed. " It's not so very nice, is it? " he asked after a while. " Not very ", we said, now pausing a long time between each nibble. Then he shouted, " I think it's awful! " and flung his portion on the fire. Ours quickly followed it. But the thought of wasted flour and potatoes damped our spirits, and we flung open door and windows to let the smell escape before Mother came.

She made very good herb beer, and we found the herbs for her. On Saturdays we started off after breakfast to pick coltsfoot, taking lunch in a carpet bag. We wandered across the fields, past our old home in the Breach, through Engine Lane and on to the railway line by Moor Green, High Park and to Watnall pit. Those walks were full of interest. Not a flower, tree or bird escaped Bert's notice, and he found wonderful adventure in seeing the first celandine or early violet. Coming home weary and footsore, we could see our home miles away on the hill. No wonder my father's feet dragged up it in heavy pit boots after a hard day's work.

One day when Bert came home from school he was tremendously excited. A friend, Pussy Templeman, had promised him two tame white rats. Could he have them? Mother reluctantly gave consent, and father rigged up a big wooden box in the scullery. One morning we were dismayed to find a large family of baby rats, and father had the unpleasant job of getting rid of them. The rats were very tame and soon knew our voices. They loved to run all over us, among my long hair and under Bert's waistcoat — down his sleeves and into his pockets to sleep. Once we were playing with them in the yard when a neighbour, an old Irishwoman, came to the gate with a pail of water, and as she passed, one of the rats suddenly ran out of my long hair and the other popped its head out of Bert's shirt-front. Poor Mrs. May had the shock of her life. Down went the pail of water, up went her arms, and with a shriek of " Rots! deary me, Rots! " she fled indoors. Long after we parted with our pets she shook her head at Mother, and marvelled at the way " Rots " were allowed to run about us.

Bert loved all animals. We had given our rats away when an adorable little black and white smooth-haired terrier was brought from Nottingham to be reared for one of our uncles. We begged to be allowed to take him to bed for the first night. Mother wouldn't hear of it, so after putting him on the sofa we went upstairs, but not to sleep. No sooner was the rascal left alone than he set up piteous howls, and we shed tears in sympathy. At last Bert could stand it no longer, and whispering, " I'm going to fetch him up here, " he crept downstairs and quietly brought the wretched little fellow to bed, where he cuddled close to him and slept soundly until morning, when we hurried down and put him back on the sofa before mother was up.

At breakfast we had a fierce argument about his name. Emily and I thought Toby or Spot, or some such common enough name would do, but Bert wouldn't accept them. He decided that it should be Rex, because the terrier was king of our hearts, and Rex it was. Even Mother, with her many anxieties, although she was furious when he pulled her things to pieces and tore our stockings when we raced pell-mell down the fields and grabbed at our legs, began to love him. It was a tragic day when the uncle came for him, and we all cried and hated him because he spoke so roughly to the little fellow.

In spite of the fact that luxuries of any

kind were unknown to us, much of our early life was very happy, and many days are fixed in my memory, days of such care-free joy with Bert that I know I can never experience again. It seemed inevitable that Bert should spend his life creating things. He was never content to copy others, and perhaps found more pleasure in inventing games than in playing them.

We had to create our happiness. There was little ready made about us. We were always conscious of poverty and the endless struggle for bread. Perhaps many other children of mining folk knew frequently enough that they had not enough to eat. We were conscious of more. The anxieties of our mother were shared by us. She never concealed the fact that she had not enough money to clothe and feed us as adequately as she wished. The sight of Father coming up the field at midday took all the pleasure from our games. It meant that on Friday night he would be short of half a day's pay. I don't remember him giving mother more than thirty five shillings a week. So much was rare. The usual amount was twenty five. The rent was five shilling and rates were extra. She baked the bread, made what clothes she could for us and schemed day and night so that we should have enough to eat. It was the terrible indignity of such poverty that embittered my brother so much.

I wonder if many children of wealthier homes got as much real joy as we did out of Christmas preparations. The most exciting days were when we searched for holly for the kissing bunch. (We never had a Christmas tree). Sometimes we tramped miles to find berried branches, but often had to be content with small pieces tied into a large bunch, which we hung from a hook in the ceiling. Then out came the wooden box containing the treasures we had saved for years. I remember the chief decoration was an angel with feathery wings, keeping guard over the glistening balls, apples and other shining things. Each picture was decorated with a sprig of holly, and a bunch of misletoe was hung by Bert in some secret spot. We plucked the duck or goose, while Mother made mince-pies. Whatever the circumstances our stockings were always well filled, with a sugar pig and mince-pie at the top. Usually we each had a book or some small toy. Once my chief present was a suite of doll's furniture, while Bert had a delightful farmyard with fowls possessing real feathers

BRINSLEY PIT

and red flannel combs. The " Chatterbox " and the " Prize " had never given us such happiness, and the games we played were weird and wonderful.

For breakfast on Christmas morning there was a pork pie with a piece of holly stuck in the top. The table would not have been complete without it. At night we had our party, and crowds of young folk came. Until the death of Ernest, Mother always took part in our games and joined in our songs. He had been the life and soul of them. After he died she would stay in the kitchen in her rocking chair, pretending to read. We knew where her thoughts were, and it always cast a shadow over the fun.

A few years after the death of Ernest we went to live in Lynn Croft, to a house owned by friends. The street was not so

43

pleasant as the one we had left, but there was a lovely garden with a field at the end of it. Mother was happy here amongst the flowers. She knew every one.

At this house there was a large garret, and here one Christmas Eve we arranged a dance. Bert said we must wax the floor, and persuaded Mother to give us two candles, which we shredded and rubbed into the wood by sliding about for half an hour or so. We decorated the beams with Chinese lanterns, hung a fancy curtain here and there, and put bits of misletoe wherever there was room.

There were about eight couples. For music we depended on George, a school friend, and Eddie (who is now my husband). George's repertoire was quite varied, and we managed the polka, waltz, minuet and even lancers with great enthusiasm. But as poor Eddie could only play from memory the waltz - " Love's Golden Dream Is O'er ", we had Love's Golden Dream for waltz, polka, and valeta, until perspiration dropped from the end of the violinist's nose.

All the girls loved to dance with Bert. His movements were so light. It was a thrilling moment when a lantern caught fire, and we nearly blew our heads off and stamped through the floor in putting it out.

Someone suggested ghost stories, and we trooped downstairs into the parlour, put out the light and gathered round the fire.

Bert, of course, told the tale, plunging into a ghastly adventure until our hair nearly stood on end. When he reached the most thrilling point he hesitated. Suddenly there was a most horrible banging and clattering just outside the door. We shrieked with terror and sat with palpitating hearts, and in marched George, who had been instructed by Bert to create the pandemonium at the critical moment, and who, strange to say, had not been missed. Mother sat in the kitchen alone, but content because we were happy.

When Bert was about sixteen we met the Chambers family at Hagg's Farm, the Willey Farm of " Sons and Lovers ", the home of Miriam.

We spent many days in the country, and to Bert everything in the fields and woods was familiar. An Easter ramble I shall never forget was to Wingfield Manor, a lovely ruin near Matlock in the Derbyshire hills. It was a beautiful sunny Monday. We were up early, and packed lunches of veal sandwiches and hot cross buns. At nine o'clock the Hagg's farm party arrived and we set off — four boys and three girls. We took the train to Alfreton, and Bert, who liked old buildings, said we must look round the church. He took a great deal of interest in Architecture. But when we saw the Easter decorations, masses of daffodils, narcissus and Lent Lilies, he said we must sing a hymn or two, and threatened awful punishments if anyone laughed or treated the occasion lightly. I played the organ and we sang. After the boys had explored the belfry we set off for Wingfield.

Nothing escaped my brother's notice on the way, however deep in conversation he might be. He was the first to see the baby rabbit or cock-pheasant, the first primrose, or the fascinating male and female flowers of the larch.

At last we saw the ruins high up on a grassy slope. Bert loved the old place with its turrets and lonely crypt. Wallflowers grew among the stonework of the tower, and we climbed to the top to look over the deep lined face of Derbyshire. We reviled Cromwell and his men, who had destroyed the Manor, and spent a great deal of sympathy on Mary Queen of Scots who was imprisoned there.

We went on to Crich Stand, where a tower stands on an immense cliff near a small village. It is said that on a fine day

one can see Lincoln Cathedral from the top
of the tower. The beautiful valley of the
Derwent lies below.

After passing through Holloway and
Lea (the home of Florence Nightingale),
we came to Whatstandswell, where we
discovered we were terribly hungry. Lunch
had been eaten long ago. When we had set
aside our train fare from Ambergate to
Langley Mill we pooled the remainder of
the money. It amounted to sevenpence.
" Now ", said Bert, who was always the
leader and was never ruffled by emergency
" We must get some bread and butter from
a cottage ". It was astonishing how much
he got for so little. We drank from a
spring. My brother's descriptions of the
country in his novels and articles show how

deeply he felt about it, and how much he knew of it.

Hagg's farm was about three miles from Eastwood — a lovely walk past Moorgreen Reservoir, over fields, and through a little wood carpeted in spring with forget-me-nots. The farm house was low and long and the outbuildings adjoined it. There was a little strip of garden at the front, a gate separating it from the wood. At the back was a stack yard. Beyond it the fields stretched to Felley Mill (the Strelley Mill of " The White Peacock "). The three sons helped their father. The two daughters were school teachers. We climbed the apple trees, see-sawed, played hide and seek in the grain, and Bert tried his hand at milking cows.

50

STRELLEY MILL ("THE WHITE PEACOCK").

In winter when work was finished we gathered round the piano in the parlour, and sang songs from a book, which Bert had given to me, and played charades.

Mr. Chambers rented two fine mowing fields opposite Greasley church, and each year Bert helped with the haymaking, going early in the morning and working until after sundown. He could drive the cutting machines and load as well as the others, and had a wonderful amount of energy. While they worked we prepared huge quantities of bread and meat and currant-pies by the shady hedge side. One night, Bert and George, one of the sons, decided to sleep by a haystack, but were joined in the early hours by a tramp, whose company wasn't exactly peaceful. They kept to their beds after that. This part of the country is described by my brother in " Love Among the Haystacks ".

Some of our happiest hours were spent at our old piano with its faded green silk front. It had to be touched gently to bring out the tinkling notes. Bert bought me Chopin waltzes, music by Tschaikowsky and Brahms, Boosey's song books, and opera selections. He could not play but sat by my side for hours at a time encouraging me to practise difficult pieces. Sometimes they seemed beyond me and I was often on the verge of tears, begging to be left alone, but he insisted that I should persevere and hummed the air while I struggled with its complications. We sang duets —

Mendelssohn's " Maybells and Flowers ",
" The Passage Bird's Farewell ", and
Rubenstein's " Song of the Birds ", but
no-one else heard them. There were sing-
songs at Hagg's Farm but our duets were
never given there. He only sang them for
his and my amusement.

Then he decided he would learn to play
the piano. He could read music easily and
thought he could master the rest as effort-
lessly as he painted and wrote. I remember
how he shut himself in the front room and
for half an hour or so we heard him
labouring with simple scales and exercises.
Then came a loud crash of keys and an
exasperated young man stalked into the
kitchen. His patience was exhausted and
he refused to strum his fingers off over
" beastly scales " any longer. He never

tried again and was content to sit with me and hum and sing.

Bert and I often went to the home of " The Lost Girl ". The cinema described in that novel actually existed, and when Alvina (her real name was Florence) was ill, I played the piano for her during a performance. Miss Wright, the Miss Frost of the book, was a splendid woman who stayed with the family until she died. She made a comfortable living by teaching music. She taught both my sister Emily and me. " Throttle Ha' penny " was the name by which we all knew the little coal-pit at Hill-top, Eastwood. Many people invested money in it and lost. Knarborough is, of course, Nottingham, and Lumley is Langley Mill. The " Moon and Stars Inn " is the

" Sun Inn " at Eastwood. The village is much
changed since those days. New houses and
shops have sprung up all over it, and many
of the people we knew so well have gone.
Walker Street is not very different, excepting
that the houses have become shabby and
the lovely mezerum tree is missing from our
front garden. The old ash tree has been
cut down, but there is still a splendid view
over the valley. Lynn Croft seems even
more drab, and the field at the bottom of
our garden has been cultivated by a
nurseryman. The Breach has grown more
ugly with age, and not many of the people
we knew remain.

Bert would never tolerate vulgarity and
dirty stories. He was gentle to human beings
and animals. He satirised men and women

55

whom he had known as a boy, but pitied rather than hated those who caused him pain. Cruelty revolted him. One day he came home sick because he had to dissect parts of a frog at school.

My first post as a teacher was at Somercotes near Alfreton, when I was nineteen. Later I taught at Eastwood Elementary School, until I married when I was twenty six. Emily was married when She was twenty-two, and she and George are still living.

My brother was never the great writer and artist to me. He was the simple, kind and loving brother who took me by the hand to school and always studied my welfare and happiness until he died. Like another, great English writer who came from

Nottinghamshire, Lord Byron, he was reviled by his own people. He never came back to live among them. One day he will come home to them in his books, and they will learn the truth about him and understand his life; and, what is perhaps more important, they will learn a little truth about themselves. "

The young Lawrences attended the Congregational Chapel three times on Sunday, morning and evening service, and Sunday School. Ada sang in the choir. They also belonged to the Band of Hope and signed the pledge, and sang " There's a serpent in the glass dash it down! " and " Dare to be a Daniel, dare to stand alone ", with fervent enthusiasm. His elders little realised how Bert Lawrence would dare to

stand alone, and for what cause. A short
time before his death he wrote an article in
which he spoke about the beauty of some of
the hymns he sang. He loved the hymn
" Awake my soul and with the sun — " there
was poetry in it. He learnt things easily,
and did not dislike school.

Mr Lawrence assumed that the boys
would go down the pit and that the girls
would become domestic servants. But the
mother was determined that her sons
should not be like their father, and that
her daughters should not bear burdens like
hers. The father reacted to the rather
snobbish attitude of his children by living
up to their ideas about him. He was an
independant fellow, and paid little respect
to his bosses. He was a good workman,
received his money, and considered the

contract between them ended there. He probably told them to go to Hell from time to time. At any rate he lost one good stall after another, and his wages dropped accordingly. Bert loathed the smell of pit dirt and his father's crude habits, which were gradually cultivated to annoy his " superior " children. But he respected his young son, and was even afraid of him, perhaps because he realised that the boy saw through the veneer of vulgarity and despised his lack of self-respect.

When he was thirteen Bert won a scholarship and went to Nottingham High School. He travelled to and fro by train and spent three years there. He was not very much interested in the other boys' pleasures, and a term report shows what one might expect. Those who objected to the recent exhibition of his pictures will be glad to know that his drawing in 1898 was " quite satisfactory ", that he was very diligent, and that his conduct was " very good ".

NOTTINGHAM HIGH SCHOOL.

XMAS, Term., 1898.   Shell Form.

Form Work	Number of Boys.	Place 2. Very satisfactory.
English	17	2. Good.
French	17	1. Very good.
German	17	1. Good.
Scripture	17	11. Fair.
Writing	47	4. Very good.
Drawing	33	12. Quite satisfactory.
Science	78	54. Moderate.
Mathematics	43 Arith. 1) He works very Alg. 3) intelligently.	
Diligence - Very good.		
Conduct - Very good.		
Times late — —.		
Times detained — —.		
Times absent — —.		
Excuses brought — —.		

In August, 1906, he went to Mablethorpe for a holiday, and as far as is known the following page from a diary is the earliest piece of work by him that has not been destroyed.

From a Diary.   9 Aug., 1906.
Wednesday.

" Walked to Theddlethorpe — the rushes, reeds and the blue butterfly, the countryside and charming farms and cottages. Fancy trekking hence from Hagg's! The trippers down to Mablethorpe in the haywaggon, and the sheep whose faces and legs gleam white as they trot south. Came at last to Theddlethorpe St. Helens, whose post office is kept by Hephzibah Lingard.

Theddlethorpe St. Helens church — its beautiful situation seen from the field. The

Vicar and his scandal. Gathered watercress from the dyke, and passed the reading room and the old farm yard whose sheds are leaning, while the various yards are enclosed by old decaying board fences, all covered with lichen.

All Saints — the old patched exterior and white vicarage. Turkeys running the yard. Interior, the strange vestry and brasses. Old slanting pews and coalyard inside church. The quaint fences and gargoyles of exterior.

On the road again. Look in at a tall black mill, climb steps, watch barley meal grinding. How afraid we were that the sails would strike us, although they were above our heads.

Next called at Susannah Stone's in a long low thatched cottage. Drank beer and ate bread and great pieces of red cheese in kitchen, seated in cornered chair. On again — arrived home much tired.

Afternoon. — The lifeboat launched. A rocket went up — boat struggled up pull-over and dashed down sands at last (cork jackets scrambled in and began raising masts, etc.). The horses plunge and swing boat round before men get in. Speeches from two men while sails are being pulled up, and one merry-faced old fellow says last word. The tide drives us back and the horses kick up the water. Ready after some time waiting, whipping of horse by the brown-faced country men on backs and by the strong, big, phlegmatic farmer-looking man at heads. Horses rear and struggle, but are disunited. At last turned round to pull

64

inland — two more added — shaft snaps.
Plunge and rear to no purpose — blue-jacks
dismount and pull — at last away it goes
for a few yards. Horses now reversed
go dashing into the sea, splashing the
bare feet of their drivers, and running
on until they are up to the thighs
— then turned round. The stays are loosed,
and the boat glides beautifully on to the
water, then rises and falls in the waves like
a child in its mother's arms. Twelve oars
stand out simultaneously and sweep the sea.
The wind fills the brown sails, and away
she glides like a live thing, the sun burning
on her red sails."

Lawrence began to paint when he was
fifteen or sixteen. He received his only

lesson fron Mr. Parkinson, the designer at a Langley Mill pottery factory. He bought plaques and painted floral designs on them in water colours, and decorated fire screens. He was twenty three when his mother died and during the last few days of her life sat in her bedroom and worked with a drawing board across his knees. He found a magazine containing reproductions of Greiffenhagen and Corot, and copied them. In " Sons and Lovers " he describes Paul Morel painting " The Idyll ". It was his own experience. He finished it at Croydon and gave it with eight other pictures, which are reproduced in this book, to his sister Ada as a wedding present. He made two copies of " The Idyll ", giving the other to a girl friend. These are his earliest pictures. In a Nottingham University College notebook containing his notes on botany and drawings of specimens he also wrote his first poems. Years later in a letter-postcard to Ada he refers to this old little college notebook " in which I have written my poems — the first I ever wrote ".

Among them are these lines on Corot, thoughts which probably came to him while he was copying the artist's work at Lynn Croft.

COROT

The music of music is stillness, you birds,
Cease a moment in reverence
And listen, oh Everything, listen, for words
Foil the sense.

The trees rise tall and taller, lifted
On the subtle rush of the cool grey flame
That issuing out of the moon has sifted
The spirit from each leaf's frame.

67

For the trailing, leisurely rapture of life
Drifts dimly forward easily hidden
By noise of small birds singing: fife
Of noisy birds, be you chidden.

The grey phosphorescent, pellucid advance
Of the luminous Purpose of God shines out
Where the lofty trees athwart stream perchance
Shake flakes of its meaning about.

The subtle, steady rush of the whole
Gray foam-fringe of advancing God
As he silently sweeps to his somewhere, his goal,
Is heard in the grass of the sod.

Is heard in the windless whisper of leaves,
In the far-off labour of men in the field
In the down-ward drooping flimsy sheaves
Of cloud, the morn skies yield.

In the tapping haste of a fallen leaf
In the flapping of red-roof smoke, and the small
Footstepping tap of men beneath
These trees so huge and tall.

For what can all sharp-rimmed substance but
                                    [catch
In a backward ripple God's progress, reveal
For a moment his great direction, scratch
A spark beneath his wheel.

Since God sweeps onward dim and vast
Down every channelled vein of man
Or leaf, and his passing shadow is cast
On each face for us to scan.

Then listen, for silence is not lonely,
Imitate the magnificent trees
That speak no word of their rapture, but only
Breathe largely the Luminous breeze.

Although Lawrence inherited his father's
independent spirit, he did not inherit his
physical strength. He became dangerously ill
with pneumonia, by which he was attacked
several times during his youth. There is

69

little doubt that this made way for consumption, against which he struggled with astonishing fortitude.

When he left the High School he saw an advertisement for a youth by Messrs. Haywood, a Nottingham firm of surgical goods manufacturers. Ernest, who was experienced in business matters, wrote this application for him:

" Gentlemen,

" In reply to your ad. in today's G. (the ' Nottingham Guardian ') for a junior clerk, I beg to place my services at your disposal. I am sixteen years of age, and have just completed three years' course at the Nottingham High School. Although I have not had any business experience in accounts yet, I studied book-keeping and obtained

NETHERMERE

two prizes for Mathematics, as well as one for French and German.

" If desired, I shall be pleased to furnish you with the highest references as to character and ability, both from my late masters and the Minister in this town.

" Should you favour me with the appointment I would always endeavour to merit the confidence you place in me. Trusting to receive your favourable reply,

" I beg to remain, Gentlemen,

    " Yours obediently,

    " D. H. Lawrence ".

He got the job, and was paid about thirteen shillings a week. He has described the place in " Sons and Lovers ". Clara and her husband are fictitious characters: the rest is true. After a year at Haywood's,

Bert went to the British School at Eastwood as a pupil teacher. Ada also became a pupil teacher, and they attended a training centre at Ilkeston. He was first in all England and Wales in the Uncertificated Teachers Examination. When he was eighteen he went to Nottingham University College to take a certificate. This meant a good deal of sacrifice by his mother, who made as much of the children's clothing as she could. Fees and railway fares had to be paid. During this time he began to write " The White Peacock ".

Then his mother developed cancer, and died in 1910. Before her death a special copy of " The White Peacock " was printed, so that she might read it. How much he loved her is plain to see in " Sons and Lovers, " although she hated Miriam because she was afraid of losing him.

72

THE RAM INN. ("THE WHITE PEACOCK").

Paul Morel stood in the room where his mother lay dead.

" The room was cold, that had been warm for so long. Flowers, bottles, plates, all sick-room litter was taken away; everything was harsh and austere. She lay raised on the bed, the sweep of the sheet from the raised feet was like a clean curve of snow, so silent. She lay like a maiden asleep. With his candle in his hand, he bent over her. She lay like a girl asleep and dreaming of her love. The mouth was a little open, as if wondering from the suffering, but her face was young, her brow clear and white as if life had never touched it. He looked again at the eyebrows, at the small winsome nose a bit on one side. She was young again. Only the hair as it arched so beautifully from her temples was mixed with silver, and the two simple plaits that lay on her shoulders were filigree of silver and brown. She would wake up. She would lift her eyelids. She was with him still. He bent and kissed her passionately. But there was coldness against his mouth. He bit his lip with horror. Looking at her, he felt he could never, never let her go. No! He stroked the hair from her temples. That, too, was cold. He saw the mouth so dumb and wondering at the hurt. Then he crouched on the floor whispering to her: ' Mother, Mother! ' ".

And that he loved and knew the country intimately is shown in " The White Peacock ", perhaps more than in any other of his novels. He writes of Hagg's Farm:

HAGG's FARM - THE HOME OF MIRIAM.

" I was born in September, and love it best of all the months. There is no heat, no hurry, no thirst and weariness in corn harvest as there is in the hay. If the season is late, as is usual with us, then mid-September sees the corn still standing in stook. The mornings come slowly. The earth is like a woman married and fading; she does not leap up with a laugh for the first fresh kiss of dawn, but slowly, quietly, unexpectantly lies watching the waking of each new day. The blue mist, like memory in the eyes of a neglected wife, never goes from the wooded hill, and only at noon creeps from the near hedges. There is no bird to put a song in the throat of morning; only the crow's voice speaks during the day. Perhaps there is the regular breathing hush of the scythe, even the fretful jar of the mowing machine. But next day, in the morning, all is still again. The lying corn is wet, and when you have bound it, and lift the heavy sheaf to make the stook, the tresses of oats wreathe round each other and droop mournfully.... Afternoon is all warm and golden. Oat sheaves are lighter, they whisper to each other as they freely embrace. The long stout stubble twinkles as the foot brushes over it; the scent of the straw is sweet. When the poor, bleached sheaves are lifted out of the hedge, a spray of nodding wild raspberries is disclosed, with belated berries ready to drop; among the damp grass lush blackberries may be discovered. Then one notices that the last bell hangs from the ragged spire of foxglove. The talk is of people, an odd book; of one's hopes and the future; of Canada, where work is strenuous, but not life; where the plains are wide, and one is not lapped in a soft valley, like an apple that falls in a secluded orchard. The mist steals over the face of the warm afternoon. The tying up is all finished, and it only remains to rear up the fallen bundles into stooks. The sun sinks into a golden glow in the west. The gold turns to red, the red darkens, like a fire burning low, the sun disappears behind the bank of milky mist, purple like the pale bloom on blue plums, and we put on our coats and go home. "

During two years at the College he matriculated and took his teacher's certificate. He then obtained a position at

Davidson Road School in Croydon. During
that year he wrote a good deal — poetry
and articles and short stories. One of the
stories, which he sent to Ada, and which has
not been previously printed is included in
this book. Muriel is obviously another name
for Miriam. He met Ford Madox Hueffer
and Edward Garnett, who helped to
introduce him to editors. Some of his
work was being published in the " English
Review. " He wrote to Ada on 9 Feb. 1911:

" .... I haven't got any news. Violet Hunt
wrote me very nicely the other day and
asked me to go to the Author's Club. She's
going to hail me in the ' Chronicle ' as a
great man, God help us. I had a great long
letter from Hueffer too. He's very friendly.

COSSETHAY. (THE ROOF OF THE BRANGWEN'S COTTAGE IS ON THE LEFT).

Still in Germany you know. There's a long and good review in today's ' Morning Post ', which is a conservative, very aristocratic paper. They amuse me highly by wondering if I'm a woman.... I think I'm about sound now. George is better. He wrote me that the ' Guardian ' is stirred up on my behalf, so that Nottingham will perhaps shortly have me on its tongue, that is if whoever it is that reviews, appreciates. I shan't want to come home at Easter — folk will stare at me.... I shan't come home to Lynn Croft. I don't much want to come to Eastwood at all. Let us go away again shall we? I don't want to come to Eastwood. "

The Eastwood home was broken up and

Ada looked after her father. School work
was depressing and on 1 March he wrote:

" .... No, there is nothing I want, saving
the woman, and if you like, the black vases,
which always remind me of home: not, God
knows, that one wants too much to be
reminded thereof.... Yes, I will come home
at Easter. It would cost a lot for us to go
away, and I want to see folk. But I hate
Eastwood abominably, and I should be glad
if it were puffed off the face of the earth.
I have now done five (pictures). I believe
the book (' The White Peacock ') is doing
moderately well. It will not make me much

money, and Heaven alone knows at that rate when I shall be able to settle down. But no matter. What one can do for two months one can do 'ad infinitum'. Sometimes I have a fit of horror which is very hard to put up with. It is often a case of living by sheer effort — we pay very heavily for this boon of living. "

Lawrence was never self-satisfied and criticised his own work more severely than any other. He was lonely and in another letter said:

12 Colworth Rd., 8 March 1911.

" .... I have to fairly kick myself towards

81

a sheet of note-paper. You are moving tomorrow. Oh, I do hope it will all be a success. If not you'll have to split again, and send father into digs. It is very wearying and bothersome....

" I am sorry you are still so troubled. Oh dear, there's nothing to do but grin and bear it. And don't meddle with religion. I would leave all that alone if I were you, and try to occupy myself fully in the present. At present I find the only antidote is work. Heavens, how I do but slog! It gets the days over, at any rate. I wish we were nearer to be company. I find that folks aren't company for me: I am as much alone with the friends here as if I were solitary. But how used one gets to a lonely life. I'm sure I've now no intimate friends here, and I don't want any. I am sufficient unto myself, and prefer to be

82

left alone.... The publisher has not written to me. I told you I had said to him I would not have the Siegmund book * published. That has offended him, I suppose. I don't care a rap. He can go to the devil. "

Louie, who is mentioned in a letter dated 27 March, was a girl with whom he was in love. The copy of Greiffenhagen's " Idyll ", which he sent to Ada, is, of course, described in " Son and Lovers ".

" It's not long to Easter, " he wrote. " I'm glad for the sake of the holiday and of seeing some of my own people. But I don't want to come to Eastwood. You'll not get me in the town much, I can tell you..... I've

---

* " The Trespasser ".

painted you a little 'Idyll', about 14 — " 7 ". Do you remember? I began to draw it the night mother died, and I said I should never finish it. Now I've done a big one for Louie, and a little one for you. It looks nice.... In the things that matter one has to be alone in this life, or nearly alone. I never say anything to anybody but sometimes I can hardly swallow the meals. And there is no refuge from one's own thoughts day after day. It's no good writing in this strain, however. Bear a thing as if it weren't there — that's the only way. Folk hate you to be miserable, and to make them a bit miserable.... School goes quietly. I often go to the boss for an evening. "

At this time, Ada, who had been a member

84

of the Chapel choir for years, was finding
that the religious creed in which she had
been brought up, did not satisfy her
intelligence. She wrote to Bert about her
difficulties. He had already formed his own
ideas about creeds and faiths. He wrote to
her:

" 12 Colworth Rd.

" Addiscombe, Croydon.

" 9 April, 1911.

" I am sorry more than I can tell to find
you going through the torment of religious
unbelief: it is so hard to bear, especially
now. However, it seems to me like this:
Jehovah is the Jew's idea of God not ours.
Christ was infinitely good, but mortal as we.

There still remains a God, but not a personal God: a vast, shimmering impulse which waves onwards towards some end, I don't know what — taking no regard of the little individual, but taking regard for humanity. When we die, like rain-drops falling back again into the sea, we fall back into the big, shimmering sea of unorganised life which we call God. We are lost as individuals, yet we count in the whole. It requires a lot of pain and courage to come to discover one's own creed, and quite as much to continue in lonely faith. Would you like a book or two of philosophy? or will you merely battle out your own ideas? I would still go to chapel if it did me any good. I shall go myself, when I am married. Whatever name one gives Him in worship we all strive towards the same God, so we be generous hearted:

THE COTTAGE OF WILL AND ANNA BRANGWEN AT COSSETHAY.

Christians, Buddhists, Mrs. Dax, me, we all stretch our hands in the same direction. What does it matter the name we cry? It is a fine thing to establish one's own religion in one's heart, not to be dependent on tradition and second-hand ideals. Life will seem to you, later, not a lesser, but a greater thing. This which is a great torment now, will be a noble thing to you later on. Let us talk, if you feel like it, when I come home. "

He wrote again on 26 April:

" .... My dear - I don't know what to say to you. There is nothing to do with life but to let it run, and it's a very bitter thing, but it's also wonderful. You never know what'll happen next. Life is full of wonder and surprise, and mostly pain.

87

But never mind, the tragic is the most holding, the most vital thing in life and as I say, the lesson is to learn to live alone.... I never want Lou to understand how relentlessly tragic life is — not that. But I want her not to jar on me by gawkishness, and that she must learn. She may give me up, I shall not her. I should be very sorry if she did. But she can take her own way in it. Try when you are feeling very irritable and bitter with folk, to remember " Ah well they don't understand — if they did, this cruelty for them also ". It is well for the balance of the world that it be mostly blind to the tragic issue. It is best so far and perhaps — but I know what horrible pain it is for you: and unfortunately, it's a thing we can't bear vicariously. I wish we could. I never pass long without thinking of you.

THE MARSH FARM ("THE RAINBOW").

Don't judge me by exterior. It is all rattle,
like dead leaves blown along the road. I
have sent Mrs. Hopkin some of MacLeod's
books which I want you particularly to
read.... They are tragedies, but all great
works are. Tragedy is beautiful also. This
is my creed. But sometimes also it leaves
me full of misery. Never mind, my dear. "
" I am very sorry father is proving such
a nuisance to you. Never mind, he will be
much humbler when he has not got his own
house to be boss in. Let him eat a bit of the
bread of humility. It is astonishing how
hard and bitter I feel towards him.

" I am tired of life being so ugly and
cruel. How I long for it to turn pleasant.
It makes my soul heave with distaste to see
it so harsh and brutal. I'm glad you like
Louie. When she is a bit older she'll be

more understanding. Remember she's seen nothing whatever of the horror of life, and we've been bred up in its presence: with father. It makes a great difference.... I've been painting lately. I've not written much. I find I can't. The publisher has not written to me lately. He owes me a letter. I believe the 'Peacock' is going pretty well. Did you see that rageous review in the 'Daily News?' It amused me. I'd upset *that* man whoever he was, hadn't I? But he acknowledged my power very sincerely. People here are very nice at school and everywhere. I shall stop on at Croydon I think, yet awhile. It was Louie's birthday on Monday, and I didn't know. I've bought her rather a pretty brooch of paste brilliants. Don't be jealous of her. She hasn't any space in *your* part of me. You and I — there are

90

some things which we shall share we alone, all our lives.... you are my own *real* relative in the world — only you. I am yours: is it not so? I don't care much about the 'Peacock' really I don't. And I am going to suppress the Siegmund book. It is better so. "

Later in the year he was happier. The Garnetts and Violet Hunt (who wrote for the " Daily Chronicle ") were very kind to him, but he couldn't write as he wished and work hard in school all day as well. The following are extracts from letters written between 17 Feb. and 8 Nov.

" .... You know I'm going to Garnett's this weekend. It'll be nice, I think. I heard from Hueffer in Germany the other day.

He's married Violet Hunt over there. She writes me very sweetly. I shall visit her in London.... I had such a nice letter last night from Ireland, from an admirer of the 'Peacock'. The lady said that Mrs. Thurston, the lady novelist who died suddenly in Ireland, had spoken to her so warmly and deeply of the book — said it was such a beautiful book and had moved her so much. It made me feel a bit queer. " .... If you are short you will consider my money as yours. I'm not married yet.

" I had such a ripping time at Garnett's. The Cearne is a big cottage built in the 15th century style, and you'd think it was a fine old farmhouse. Everything old, thick blue earthenware, stone jugs for the beer, a great wood fire in the open hearth in the ingle-

nook and all buried in the middle of a
wood, hard to find. I like Garnett ever so
much. I shall go and stay with him again
soon. Hueffer has married Violet Hunt in
Germany. They'll be home soon, living in
her house. I shall go and see them next
week, I think.

" Garnett is going to get my verses
published, and perhaps a vol. of plays in
Spring. I am terribly busy.

" I've got to go and lunch with Wm.
Heinemann on Friday. The agreement is
a yearly one. I should draw my cheque in
February. I could have it now, but I think
I shall wait. I wonder what the little bear
wants with me now.

" .... And these verses. Garnett put them
in last week's ' Nation ' all unknown to me
I am pleased to get a footing in " the

Nation ". It is a sixpenny weekly of very
good standing. I am afraid you will not
care much for the verses. The ' Violets '
is printed all wrong. You see I had
no proofs or anything. Things are going
very slowly down here. I don't get on very
well with my writing: shall have to buck up.
I shall be going to Garnett's again, and Scott
James the Editor of the ' Daily News ' will be
there. He may do me some good. I want to
leave school now as soon as I can. There is
a review by me in the ' English ' of this
month. "

One wonders what would have been said
by his newspaper enemies if he had decided
to become a schoolmaster again after the
publication of " Lady Chatterley's Lover "

D. H. LAWRENCE

an early Portrait.

One can imagine the Minister of Education being warned, threatened, and instructed that Mr. Lawrence must not set foot in an English school. When he left Davidson Road Mr. P. F. Smith, the Headmaster gave him this testimonial:

" Mr. D. H. Lawrence has been a member of the staff of the above school for the last two years, during which period he has been successively responsible for the instruction of Standards V, VI, and VII. He has also particularly directed the art training of the upper divisions, has to a great extent influenced the science teaching of the whole school, and has had considerable opportunity of observing the educational methods in operation in the lower classes. The school is one of the largest and most completely equipped buildings in South London, full provision having been made for technical instruction, in addition to the ordinary school subjects. An exhaustive and highly creditable report has recently been issued by the Board of Education, embodying the opinions of H. M. Inspectors upon the work of the department, which has now been recommended to my education authorities and to specialists as worthy of their consideration. To this very satisfactory result the work of Mr. Lawrence has greatly contributed, the subjects under his control being highly recommended. To the above testimony it will scarcely be necessary to add that as an instructor I have no hesitation in stating that Mr. Lawrence is most successful. His methods are wholly modern, and have the great merit that they are particularly adapted to obtain results in face of the limitations imposed by the elementary school curriculum. Mr. Lawrence is thoroughly in sympathy with his pupils, and possesses their entire regard, respect and confidence. Discipline on the highest plane naturally follows, and I am convinced that his genial manners and his well conceived methods of obtaining ready obedience in his class, could be extended with the greatest success to any school placed under his direction. I am sure that any Education Authority could place the greatest confidence in Mr. Lawrence, and that any duties undertaken by him would be fully, faithfully, and zealously attempted. "

James Smyth, the Clerk to the Education Committee wrote:

" Mr. David Herbert Lawrence entered

the service of my committee as a trained certificated assistant teacher in October, 1906, and has since that date carried out his duties to the entire satisfaction of the committee. Mr. Lawrence is an excellent teacher, resourceful and intelligent in his methods, a sympathetic and capable disciplinarian, and the results of his work, as evidenced by the progress of his pupils, have always been of an eminently satisfactory nature. "

From the time when he left school until his death he lived by his writing. He never returned to live in Eastwood, although during the war he went with his wife to Mountain Cottage at Middleton-in Wirksworth in the Derbyshire Hills, and

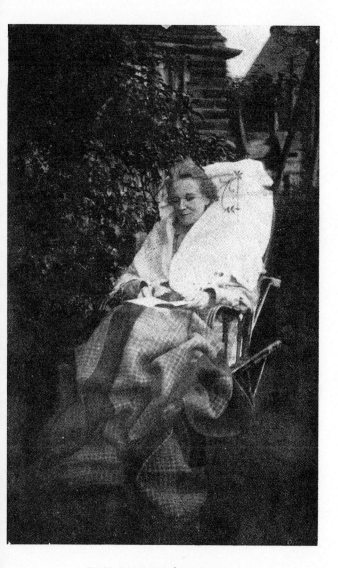

D. H. LAWRENCE'S MOTHER.

stayed with Ada at her home in Ripley. But his mind never wandered long from the Midlands. " Lady Chatterley's Lover " and " The Virgin and the Gipsy " have their setting there. Like Paul Morel his youth ended in " Sons and Lovers ". His mother was dead, his love for Miriam was dead. He must find new life and new ways of living.

" There was no time, only space. Who could say his mother had lived and did not live? She had been in one place, and was in another; that was all. And his soul could not leave her, wherever she was. Now she was gone abroad into the night, and he was with her still. They were together. But yet there was his body, his chest that leaned against the stile, his hands on the wooden bar. They seemed something. Where was he? one tiny upright speck of flesh, less than the ear of wheat lost in the field. He could not bear it. On every side the immense dark silence seemed pressing him, so tiny a spark, into extinction, and yet, almost nothing, he could not be extinct. Night, in which everything was lost, went reaching out beyond stars and sun. Stars and sun, a few bright grains, went spinning round for terror, and holding each other in embrace, there in a darkness that outpassed them all, and left them tiny and daunted. So much, and himself, infinitesimal, at the core a nothingness and yet not nothing.

" ' Mother! ' he whimpered ' Mother! '

" She was the only thing that held him up, himself, amid all this. And she was gone, intermingled herself. He wanted her to touch him, have him alongside with her.

" But no, he would not give in. Turning sharply, he walked toward the city's gold phosphorescence. His fists were shut, his mouth set fast. He would not take that direction, to the darkness, to follow her. He walked towards the faintly humming, glowing town, quickly. "

LETTERS
TO HIS SISTER ADA FROM 1911 TO 1930

(INCLUDING SEVERAL TO A FRIEND WHOM

HE HAD KNOWN SINCE CHILDHOOD

AND TO ADA'S SON)

D. H. LAWRENCE and HIS SISTER ADA.

Dominicushutte mit Schlegeistal Zillertal. (*sic*)
Austria 1911.

We have walked two days, and now have spent the night in this place, where one gets guides to climb the glaciers. It is quite snowy everywhere. The guides keep coming in, with edelweiss in their hats, with ice axes and ropes. It is the most beautiful view you can imagine. We have now got eight hours to go, over the mountains, to Sterzing. But don't write me till you hear from me. I don't know what address I shall have.

Garnett* (junior) is here, and a ripping fellow who is spending this time with us on his way from Moscow.... I'll write as soon as I've stopped moving.

Sterzing. Tirol.

1911.

I am staying here only till tomorrow, Sunday, then going on to Meran and then to Bozen. You might write me a letter to Bozen in Tirol (Hauptpostlagernd). Garnett and Hobson and I had a fine time crossing the mountains here. It was quite snowy. Sterzing is a charming place already quite Italian in feeling. I shall be in Bozen in

---

* David Garnett.

about a week and shall wait for letters but write at once, and tell me how father is, and everything.... How has school gone down? How are you?

Bozen 1911.

Glad to get your letter. The coat hasn't come yet. I know I'll look like a monkey on a barrel in it. I've just corrected the proofs of a fearfully exciting vol. of verse for Duckworth. I'll send you the duplicates just now.

Bozen 1911.

Thanks for the books you sent. Here's a card to wish you a happy Christmas. Try and have as jolly a time as you can. I will do the same. And give father, from me, five shillings, will you? It's too late to get it off now, but I'll send it you next week.

I have not heard from you. I'm writing father a letter....

bei Fraulein Schneeberger

Mayrhofen 138.

Zillertal

Tirol, Austria.

1911

Have walked through the mountains to this adorable place, where I shall stay two or three weeks. There is no letter from you in the Postlagernd, perhaps it is at Wolfratshausen. I am staying in a farmhouse at the foot of the mountains, just by a lovely stream, that tears along, and is as bright as glass. On Wednesday night there was quite a heavy fall of snow, only a little way up the mountains. Do let me hear how you are going on.

I am going to München tomorrow, to stay perhaps a month or so. My address will be bei Frau Dr. Taffe-Richthofen, Wolfratshausen, bei München. From there I will write to you on Saturday. Thank Emily for her letter - tell her the first part of Paul Morel is the first writing - I did it again and have the whole here - finished all but ten pages. I got the poetry and everything all right - many thanks. You must have about ruined yourself in postage. I shall come back to Waldbröl later - it's very jolly here.

Bonn. Germany. (undated)

We are going down the Rhine on a steamer
from Bonn to the Drachenfels. It's awfully
pretty - and a lovely day. You would adore
seeing these Germans - they are delicious.
Bonn is a beautiful town. I will write you
a letter quite soon.

Italy. 1912.

I got your letter the other day and a cap
from Auntie, with a nice letter, and a sponge
bag from Emily, also with a nice letter. You
wrote me in a scuffle and a hurry, and
sounded rather as if you were ordering the
washerwoman than saying nice things to me.
But the idea of a smoking jacket is quite
gorgeous only let it be of some delightful
colour, purple or crimson or cornflower

blue — nothing dull and uninteresting. I mean it, of course. And if you have not already sent it, address it to Villa Igea, Villa di Cargnano lago di Garda, Italy. I am going there on Wednesday and shall probably stay there the winter.... I'll write you a beautiful letter directly the coat comes. I've just eaten two pounds of figs, and oh Lord! Duckworth sent me fifty quid today.

Villa Igea.

Lake Garda.

Italy.

23 Sept. 1912.

I got your letter and the enclosure from the W. G.* here. This card isn't a scrap

---

* "Westminster Gazette?"

like the Villa Igea - the reality is a million times better - fearfully nice. You must make haste to get married and come for your honeymoon - I am quite well. Have just been watching them tread the wine.

Villa Igea.

24 Oct. 1912.

You will have got my letter - your card came today. I *wish* you wouldn't bother about a smoking jacket - let it go, it doesn't matter. Send me a couple of ties instead. I don't really need a cap, so don't bother. But do stop bothering about that jacket. It is an awful hardship on Eddie.

How's the weather? It has at last got colder here. The trees in front are olives. This is a very true view.

112

Villa Igea.

14 Jan., 1913.

What a shame about your bowl - but never mind, I'll buy you another. I sent you the poem-proofs off. I guess you'll hate the stuff.

Write me a letter - it is overdue.

Switzerland.

10 June. 1914.

Tonight I sleep in Aosta - tomorrow we are going on foot over the St. Bernard pass. I shall be a week or so in Switzerland, then to London. Write me a p. c. to *Interlaken,* Switzerland - poste restante, and tell me any news there is. It is very beautiful in the Alps, but cold, after Italy. In Turin yesterday there was a great strike commotion whilst we were there.

113

Hospice du Grand St. Bernard.

12 June 1914.

Today we have struggled up here from
Aosta - the last part climbing up the face of
the snow, which is more than a yard deep
here. You have no idea how beautiful it
is. Tonight I sleep in the monastery (St.
Bernard) - such a lovely little panelled room
- and tomorrow on again. I love it dearly.
Love to you and Eddie.

5, Piazza Mentana. Florence. 1918.

I had a wire from Frieda * - she has not
yet fixed up her passport - hope she won't
be long. But I'm quite happy here, in my
room over the river - have English friends
in the house, and dine with people in town.

---

* His wife.

Florence is beautiful, and full of life and plenty. I wonder how things are going with you - shall be glad to have a line. Keep this reproduction of this very famous picture - Birth of Venus.

To Miss Cooper

> Pensione Balestri
>
> 5, Piazza Mentana
>
> Florence
>
> 1918.

Here am I on my lonel-o, waiting for Frieda. My room looks on the river - quite near this bridge - but alas it rains today. It is an awful business travelling - if you come you'll have to come *train de luxe*, and have a sleeping car. I suppose I'll be here about a week, so send a line.

5, Piazza Mentana, Florence.

Sat. evening, 29 Nov., 1918.

I have just heard from Emily, so the post is beginning to go through. Frieda is coming, arrives from Switzerland on Wednesday morning at 4.0 a.m. - hope she'll have a decent journey. She has got her trunk back - though the Dutch thieves kept all the *new* stuff.... We shall stay here till Dec. 9th. - then to Rome. I will send you an address later - but letters will come on from here. Florence is very pleasant, very nice to live in - lots of English friends here. Let me know how you all are.

To his nephew. Jack Clarke.

Capri, 18 April. 1919.

Am staying here with friends for a few days - leave for Rome tomorrow or

Wednesday - then direct to Baden. I am planning to see you this summer. - What about this strike? The boats in the picture are being towed behind the steamer, to take off passengers into the Blue Grotto. Wish there was good news from England.

Spain. 20 Dec. 1919.

Picinisco is too cold - on Monday we are going to Naples and the Island of Capri: the address, C/O. Compton Mackenzie Esq. Casa Solitaria, Isola Capri, Naples. Mackenzie is a novelist - Capri will be warm. Merry Christmas.

To Miss Gertrude Cooper.

Capri, 25 Feb. 1920.

I had your letter inside Ada's tea this evening. It is as hot as June here - all the butterflies fluttering among the flowers - wish indeed you could all be here. - Lovely green tea! - Tomorrow I am going by sea to Sicily - from Naples. If I find a house we shall go over. - Tell Ada I sent two pounds to Emily for father. Do hope you're better.

Fontana Vecchia.

Taormina.

Sicily.

4 March 1920.

I have found such a charming house here in a big garden - Frieda arrives Saturday, I hope. I'll write later.

Fontana Vecchia means old fountain - the name of the house.

Syracuse. 25 April 1921.

Friends invited us down to Syracuse for

a few days - staying in this hotel. The Latomia is one of the great quarries out of which the Greeks got the stone for the town, and in which the Athenian youths died so horribly. - It's a wonderful place - quite near to Malta - which makes one feel near to England. Post all upset here.

Sicily. 1921.

We went to Sardinia to see if we liked it to live in - love it, but decide to keep Fontana Vecchia another year. Came back last night. Find the blazer fits beautifully, and looks so chic. I like it extremely. Say how much it cost as I want to pay for it. Brilliant sun, almond trees all coming into full blossom - oranges and lemons all ripe.

Have got a funny little thing for Jack.
Send tomorrow.

Sicily. 1921.

Ages since we heard from you - have you
written? I wrote you. The post is very bad.
We've both got colds, sneezing our heads
off, after going rather high up Etna, to see
the Duca di Bronte who is Nelson's
descendant and who has a castle up there -
wonderful place. Hope we shall hear soon.

To his nephew. Jack Clarke.

Sicily. 12 Jan. 1922.

I am sending you an hourglass to remind
you that you are piling up your years.

120

Here the peasants hardly ever have clocks, and they still measure an hour by the sandglass.... I hope it will arrive unbroken - trust to luck. I hope you'll have digested your Christmas pudding before you tackle your birthday cake. Your festivities tread on each other's heels. Love from Auntie Frieda and me.

Thirroul. Australia
5 June 1922.

We have taken such a nice little furnished bungalow right on the sea - we can bathe all to ourselves - like it so much. Australia is awfully nice as a country - the bit I have seen of it. But of course one does not feel one belongs to the people. Sicily especially spoils one for the new, raw countries, and their rough sort of friendly and unfriendly

121

manners.   I hope you got the ring I sent
from Perth.   Had your letter three days
ago....   You'll be thinking of summer
holidays when you get this.   Send me a line
C/O. Robert Mountsier 417 West 118 St.
New York.

Wellington. 15 Aug. 1922.

Here we are at your antipodes - don't
want to stop here though - sail this afternoon
- are on a nice boat.

Raratonga.   20 Aug. 1922.

Such a lovely island - calling next at Tahiti
- it's really almost as lovely as one expects
these South Sea Islands to be.

Tahiti - 22 August 1922.

Sail on tomorrow afternoon - hot - lovely Island - but town spoilt - don't really want to stay. But having a very good trip.

Taos. New Mexico
20 Sept. 1922.

We arrived here on the 11th - my birthday - found your letter. Many thanks, but too extravagant: F's brooch very pretty. I have been away five days motoring to the Apache Reservation to an Apache feast. It is very fine and wild out here - but we are settling in, already making jam of peaches and of wild plums that the Indians bring. I will write a letter in a day or two. Your tennis place sounds fine - glad you make nice things for yourself.

To his nephew. Jack Clarke.

Taos. New Mexico.

We are so glad to be back in the west -
it is very nice - everybody pleased to see
us, even the Indians, apparently. I simply
can't stand the big cities any more. We
haven't had a word from England since we
left - how are you all?

Oaxaca.

1922.

We are in the house, very nice and
peaceful: but Brett is staying on in the
hotel. I am getting busy again too. It is
a wonderful climate, brilliant sun all day
long: and a letter from you.

New Mexico. 10 Feb, 1923.

Had your letter at last, and you all seem

out of sorts. But don't envy me too much the sun here, with temperature 25° below freezing point at night. And no sort of life is all honey. I ordered a copy of the Dial for you, via Emily.... The winter seems long here. If we go down to Mexico City next month it will be almost tropical there.

El Paso. 21 March, 1923.

We cross the frontier into Mexico this morning - already it is hot - such a change from the snow of Del Monte.

Hotel Monte Carlo.
Uruguay.
Mexico.
March 1923.

Had quite a good journey here - Mexico

just warm enough and very free and easy, like Naples - to me much pleasanter than U. S. - we shall probably stay at least a few months, though I am not sure - I expect some friends down from Santa Fe on Tuesday - so good to get a little wine again.

New Mexico.
30 July, 1923.

Wonder why I have not heard from you - Did you get the Indian bracelet I sent for your birthday? Emily wrote so I suppose nothing is wrong. There is nothing new here. - Did you go to Wembley? I'll bet it's a wearisome place - too much of a good thing. Did baby's mocassins fit him? Work them on like a glove. The post card is the

Taos Indians ready for their race - or ritual race.

Del Monte Ranch.

New Mexico.

31 Aug., 1924.

.... The autumn is coming here—we are so high. The summer has many thunderstorms—down in Del Monte they had three horses killed, in June, by one flash. But autumn is clear and blue, hot days, cold nights with great stars settling on the mountains. Now the big clearing in front of the house is really amethyst with dark-coloured Michaelmas Daisies, not very tall, and great gold patches of wild sunflower. But it's really a hard country, not a soft flowery country, though we've had endless strange, rather fascinating flowers up here, at this height.

127

Del Monte Ranch, New Mexico.
31 August. 1924.

.... You'll be getting " The Boy in the Bush " this week. It will amuse you. Poor Molly Skinner came to England from Australia by steerage and bringing the M.S. of another novel — " Black Swans, " Alas, Martin Secker writes me that " Black Swans " is quite useless for publication as it stands. And I doubt if I want to re-write another book, or re-create it, as I did the " Boy. " I'm sorry for Molly Skinner — her hopes dashed. " Jack " in the " Boy " was her brother. She was a peasant's daughter. They're poor now. However, she'll be getting £ 60 or £ 70 this week from the " Boy ".... I suppose we shall be here five or six weeks still, then I must go

128

to Mexico to finish my Quetyalcoatl novel
(" The Plumed Serpent ").

Hotel Francia
Oaxaca, Mexico.
15 Nov. 1924.

.... We got down here all right. There
is always a certain risk in Mexico,
especially on a little narrow railway that
winds for hours and hours in a gorge. This
is a little town, lonely, way in the south,
with little rather fierce Zapotee Indians.
The climate is lovely: just like midsummer,
cloudless sun all day, and roses and tropical
flowers in full bloom. My chest had got
very raw up at the ranch: that very high
altitude. That's why we had to come South
so soon. Already it's nearly healed up.

129

The altitude here is just about 5,000 ft. They are always expecting more revolutions: it's the most unsettled country, and the most foolish politically, on the face of the earth. But I don't suppose anything will happen to affect us seriously.... The winter is so lovely here, I hope the country will stay quiet. Otherwise we shan't be able easily to get out.... One feels far away here — I want to get my Mexican novel finished if I can.

Oaxaca, 12 January, 1925.

I had your letter yesterday. — We shall probably come to England — F. and I — end of March or in April. I think we shall go up to Mexico City the first week in Feb. — so don't write here. — I've been very

busy — wish I had got this novel * done. Brett isn't coming to England — going to Del Monte — pining for the horses and the freedom. But it will be cold there....
.... Ordered copies of Theatre Arts with Hopi Snake Dance article for you and Pamela **.

Orizaba. 21 April, 1925.

I've had about enough of this — expect to sail to New York from Vera Cruz in a week's time — stay a week or two in New York, and then sail to England. I suppose we shall stay with Thomas Seltzer.

---

* " The Plumed Serpent ".
** Emily.

Kiowa Ranch C/O.

Del Monte Ranch,

Questa, New Mexico.

30 May 1925.

.... The flowers in your garden sound
wonderful, especially the auriculas and
polyanthus. I like them so much. Here,
it is so terribly dry, there are no flowers
yet, save the scarlet and yellow columbines
— they are nice. Our little garden seeds —
nasturtium, sweet-pea, etc. are only an
inch high. The nights are cold; then the
sun by day can be blazing hot. And it is
so dry, my little stream that we bring from
the gallina is half dry. I have to turn it
over the garden and over the alfalfa field,
bit by bit: irrigating. That's my job.
Then we're building a new little corral,

132

for the horses and the black cow — she is coming up on Monday.

To his nephew. Jack Clarke.

Villa Bernarda.

Spotorno. Prov. di Genova.

19 Dec. 1925.

I'm sending you a pound, but it's only ten shillings to you. I want you to buy something for your Auntie Gertie with the other ten bob.

Tell your mother I couldn't find a thing for her in that beastly Savona: except rather lovely cups and plates and things — and she has enough of those. But if she'd like some, I could get her a parcel made up.

At last it's raining a bit here: rather nice, the country is so dry. Our old Giovanni is working away, planting his garden. One day you'll have to come with your mother to see everything and *parlare italiano*.

I do hope you get this in time. Write on your Auntie Gertie's present: *From Bert and Frieda*, and do it respectably, so as not to shame us, and don't be wessel-brained, or there'll be death in the pot.

Merry Christmas to you all: don't revel too much. And for heaven's sake, I hope the green family is better.

Love from your Auntie Frieda and your ever estimable

Uncle Bert.

What have " those pore collier's boys " been doing lately?

Spotorno, Italy · 19 April, 1926.

Was glad to get your letter. I am very much better in health — getting on my own real feet again and then one can stand firm. We leave for Florence tomorrow — address Pensione Lucchesi, Lungarno Zecca. Frieda will probably go to Baden after a week, with her daughters, but I think of staying on in Italy till July. Will write from Florence.

Florence. 3 May, 1926.

Secker has been worrying me to write a travel book — and I don't want to do an ordinary travel book, just of places. So I thought I might stay here two months or so, and prepare a book on the Etruscan cities — the dead Etruscans.... At present I'm reading the Italian books on the Etruscans, getting the idea into shape.... I do hope the strike will pass quickly and the miners will feel all right about it. I feel rather bad myself about it.

Villa Mirenda. 1 June, 1926.

I wonder how your business is going now with that beastly strike. Really it's too bad they let it come to a strike: very dangerous too, because it may start a real class war, and England is the one country where that is most dangerous. I am busy here typing the German translation of "David" and painting the doors and windows.

To Miss Cooper.

Villa Mirenda

Scandicci, Florence.

5 Oct. 1926.

.... It is almost hot here — too hot to sit in the sun. And last night, the rooms being only just opened, it was so hot I could not sleep, and thought a good deal about you in Maundesley, and wished a bit of your cold wind would blow through my open window. These old villas are so massive, made of stone, that after a long spell of sunshine it takes weeks for the walls to cool off, on the south side.

It is very lovely, really — not like autumn, like summer. The peasants are bringing in the grapes, in a big wagon drawn by two big white oxen. Every hour or so they roll up with a load, to go in the big vats in the ground-floor cellars. The grapes are very sweet this year — not very big — little and round and clear, and very sweet. It will be a good wine year, even if the bulk is not enormous.... I think tomorrow Richard Aldington and Arabella are coming out to stay a little while here: hope they won't mind the hard beds. One doesn't realise how hard they are till one comes back to them.

Mirenda, 9 Oct., 1926.

That coal strike is like an insanity. Are your men going back round Ripley? I feel I daren't read any more about it, it's so

maddening stupid — I suppose Bertie *
flourishes like the green bay tree.

To Miss Cooper.

Mirenda. 18 Oct., 1926.

.... We are settling down here, in the big,
quiet rooms. It is very nice to be quite
still, to let the autumn days go by. It is
still quite hot in the middle of the day,
only misty in the mornings. But the
windows stay open day and night, and we
only wear cotton things: hot as summer. In
the woods the little wild cyclamens, pink
ones, are dotted under the leaves. I am very
fond of them. And all the time the famous

---

* A reference to Lawrence's little nephew.

139

Italian " hunters " are banging away at the little birds, sparrows, larks, finches, any little bird that flutters. They are awful fools in some respects, these people. To see a middle-aged man stalking a sparrow with as much intensity as if it were a male rhinoceros and letting bang at it with a great gun, is too much for my patience. They will offer you a string of little birds for a shilling — robins, finches, larks, even nightingales. Makes one tired.

The natives are scared because there is an epidemic of typhoid, from an infected well, two villages away. If it moves nearer, I think we shall leave for a while. No use running risks.

The days pass so quickly. I do very little work — go out for walks by myself in these hills — and talk a bit with our only neighbours — the Wilkinsons. I'll get them to take some snapshots for you, it might amuse you.... It still seems like summer — I do hope the winter will be a short one. We haven't ordered any wood yet, for firing. We cook on little charcoal fires. (At that very moment the milk boils over!).

I do hope you are getting better. I haven't heard from Ada — the thought of that coal strike is terribly depressing.

To Miss Cooper.

Villa Mirenda.

Florence.

28 Oct., 1926.

Aldous Huxley, a writer, and his wife came for the day, in their fine new car. They want me to buy their old car, which is perfectly good. But I won't bother myself learning to drive, and struggling with a machine. I've no desire to scud about the face of the country myself. It is much pleasanter to go quietly into the pinewoods and sit and do there what bit of work I do. Why rush from place to place?

Mirenda. 28 Oct., 1926.

I'm sure it's weariness beyond words, and what the miners themselves must be feeling I don't like to think. Certainly it's one of the greatest disasters that has ever happened to England.... Really people have no pep, they so easily go blank, and so young.... Let me know how you all are. I am always thinking about the strike.

To Miss Cooper.

Villa Mirenda, 23 Nov. 1926.

.... I'm in bed these two days with a cold.
We had such deluges of rain, and I got
wet coming up from Scandicci. Everything
is steamy, soggy wet, and there are great
pale-brown floods out in the Arno valley.
We can see them from the window. And
still it thunders and lightens at times —
and it is warm. We only light the stove in
the evening for the damp.

This is the time of the year I dislike
most in any country. I wish it would come
cold and a bit crisp. The town is no better
than the country, and the country isn't
much better than the town. One can only
grin and abide.

We shan't be coming to England yet.

143

I hear they have postponed the " David "
play until March, and in December are
doing my first play that I wrote while I was
still in Croydon. " The Widowing of Mrs.
Holroyd ". It is a much simpler thing to
produce on the stage than " David " so I
needn't come home for it, though I should
very much like to be there when it is done:
about the middle of December.

.... Only the other day three friends came
to lunch, through the downpour. One was
a young Russian woman about twenty-five,
I suppose. But she had got herself up so
exactly like a boy, with her Eton crop and
black jacket and narrow skirt, that I
gasped, and Giulia, our servant, called her
the signorino, the young gentleman. Why
ever a pretty girl should want to appear
just like a lad from a public school, passes

my comprehension. To me it is just repulsive. Why can't women be women — and a bit charming!

To Miss Cooper.

Villa Mirenda.

Florence.

21 Dec., 1926.

We are busy getting ready a Christmas tree for our peasants. There will be about twelve children, and I expect their parents will have to come to look. So many people work on this little estate. And the children are wild little things. They've never seen a Christmas tree, but they heard of some other English people who made one for the peasants, so they all had fits hoping we'd do one. We've got all kinds of little wooden toys from Florence, and with a few glittering things and some sweets and dates, and the candles, it'll do for them. They never get sweets or anything like that from year's end to year's end. They're very much poorer than even the really poor in England. You see, there's no money. They just live on the wine and oil and corn and vegetables of the earth, and have no wages, no cash, unless they manage to sell a barrel of wine. But this year there wasn't much. Here, the peasants are supposed to do all the work on the land, and then they take half the produce, the landlord taking the other half. But when it's a little hilly estate like this, no pasture, no cattle, all just the hard labour of wine and a bit of wheat, a few vegetables and the olives, they don't come off very well. This bit of land round the villa has to support twenty-seven peasants, counting children. In England it wouldn't support seven. But we've no idea how poorly they live — like cattle. Still they are nice, and when we give them things, they always send us back a few dried grapes, or figs, or olives.

We shall give them their Christmas tree on Friday evening at sundown. And if the twenty-seven all of them come, it'll be like Ripley fair in this salotta. The men will have to have a glass of sweet wine, and a long cigar called a Toscana, and the women get a glass of wine and a few biscuits. There will be a buzz! I wish you could be here to help. But they talk such strong dialect that even when you know Italian you have a job to follow them.

Ada couldn't see the play " David " because Bertie was ill. — I'm sorry, I should

like her to have seen it; though I believe
most of the people found it too gloomy. I
think, if it were being done again, I should
alter the end, and make it more cheerful.
Myself, I hate miserable endings, now. But
it's so long since I wrote that play.

To Miss Cooper.
Villa Mirenda, 23 Jan., 1927.

.... My God, what a fight for life! It's no
good trying to understand why these things
should be. There's no explanation. One
can only do one's best and then live or die.
One is between the hammer and the anvil.
For myself, I daren't say either have the
operation, or don't have it. It worries me
too much. You must go way down into

yourself, down till you really *feel* which would be right, to have it or not to have it. And then abide by what you feel, in your own still soul, would be the best.

Eh, one wishes things were different. But there's no help for it. One can only do one's best, and then stay brave. Don't weaken or fret — while we live, we must be game. And when we come to die, we'll die game too. Listen to the doctors carefully when they advise you. But when it comes to deciding finally, decide out of your own real self.

The days are already beginning to lengthen, and the narcissus flowers are out in the garden already: but the little white wild ones, down by the stream, aren't out yet, nor the wild crocuses. There are lots of Christmas roses wild, but they are

149

greenish, they don't come really white, so they're not so pretty.

.... We sat in the sun on the edge of the pine wood and listened to a shepherd playing a tin whistle — very badly. They make the weirdest noises, to call the sheep: grunts from the bottom of the stomach, then wildcat hisses. I suppose it takes a peculiar sound to penetrate a sheep's stupid skull. The leading sheep with the bell was called Laura: " Hoy! Laura! Hoy — a — Hoy! Grunt — squish — squee! " so the shepherd kept on at her. And she, like an old maid, munched a bit, and tripped ahead, the rest trailing after her.

The mountains, the Appenines, are covered with deep snow, and they look very beautiful, sweeping away to the north, the furthest up, at Carrara, glimmering faint and pinkish in the far, far distance. And near at hand, the country lies in the sunshine, all open and rolling, with white buildings like dots here and there, and few people. It is very different from England. One day you must come and really get to know it. On a day like today an odd butterfly comes flapping out, and there's a bee now and then. The sun is strong enough. I even saw the tail of a little lizard go whisking down a hole in the wall.

Do you remember in Lynn Croft, when we used to have autograph albums, and put verses and little paintings in them? I can remember Frances chose for somebody's:

" But human bodies are such fools
For all their colleges and schools
That when no *real* ills perplex 'em
They make enough themselves to vex 'em. "

And I think that is so true. When one
gets a job like yours on hand, one thinks
what fools people are, grousing and grizzling
and making their lives a misery for nothing,
instead of being thankful they've got off so
lightly....

I suppose they're warbling away in
Eastwood Congregational Chapel at this
moment! Do you remember, how we all
used to feel so sugary about the vesper
verse: Lord keep us safe this night, secure
from all our fears —: Then off out into
the dark, with Dicky Pogmore and the
Chambers, and all the rest. And how Alan
used to love the lumps of mince-pie from
the pantry. And Frances did her hair up
in brussel-sprouts, and made herself a
cup of Ovaltine or something of that sort!
Sometimes it seems so far off! And
sometimes it is like yesterday.

Mirenda. 16 Feb. 1927.

For a wonder we've had a week of bright sunshine, rather lovely. The flowers are coming out: under the olives all the pale-gold bubbles of winter aconites and many daisies: and I found the first wild violet and purple anemone. In the garden there are still lovely roses and many narcissi. I suppose your snowdrops are out by now.

To Miss Cooper.

Mirenda, 16 Feb., 1927.

.... It is already beginning to be spring. Under the olive trees the winter aconites, such pretty pale yellow bubbles, are all out, and many daisies: and I found the first purple anemone. I wish I could send you some, but the post makes such a fuss nowadays about parcels big or little. The wild tulips are peeping through, though they won't flower till Easter, and the grape hyacinths also are coming. We've had a week of lovely sunshine, and so far have both escaped the 'flu, thank Heaven. There's a good deal about.

Mirenda.
20 April, 1927.

— cabled today for us to go to Taos (Mexico) — but not this year! Besides, it is too expensive. I've not got any book this year to come out except the tiny vol. of " Mornings in Mexico ". So the earnings don't amount to a great deal. And now the lira has fallen to 96 to £ 1 and will probably fall lower, which makes everything much

dearer. I've not heard another word about
" David " — who is doing it or what. So its
no use making any plans.

Mirenda. 30 April, 1927.

I heard yesterday they are doing " David "
on May 22 or 23 and they want me to go as
soon as possible to help. So I ought to come
to England next week. I must decide. I
don't really want to come. It's just lovely
hot summer here. Yet I bet they'll make
a mess of that play without me.

Mirenda. 19 May, 1927.

I did really want to come to London for
" David ". But I got a beastly cold that
everybody had and then the weather

suddenly went damp hot and that gave me malaria again and I felt rotten. I'm a good bit better now, but I hate the thought of that journey. The longer I live the less I like the actual process of travelling — trains especially. So I shan't come to the play, and they can make what mess of it they like: though I believe they're doing their best.

It keeps pretty hot here. Summer has come earlier this year. But there's a great feel of thunder and electricity all the time. The flowers are very fine, the garden is all red roses, the honey-suckle is in masses, and the broom all yellow in the woods. But it is summer, when one doesn't do much but lounge around and go for little walks in the evening and morning .... I wish really I felt more solid. When one turns forty it seems as if ones old ailments attack one with a double fury. I never seem to get really free. And then one gets sort of disillusioned. I feel like turning hermit and hiding away the rest of my days away from everybody. But I suppose it is a phase, a sort of psychic change of life many men go through after forty. I wish it would hurry up and get over and leave me feeling more or less myself. I'm glad you're busy in the shop, there's nothing like being occupied in this disintegrating world.

To Miss Cooper.

Mirenda, 19 May, 1927.

.... Now Ada says you are walking about a bit and going back to Maundesley. How marvellous that is. At last you are really on the way home to Ripley and a decent life. It seems a miracle: it is a miracle: almost a resurrection. You'll be in time for the end of spring and the coming summer — how splendid it will be, to be in the world again, and able to appreciate it all. Men and nature work wonders between them — and the will to live is a miracle in itself.... It's full blazing summer here — some of the hay is already cut and cocked up — the garden fairly blazes with red roses — they smell so sweet — and the fireflies go winking round under the olives and among the flowers at night like lost souls — and by the pools toads croak and bark like dogs. It's really summer — peas and beans and asparagus in full swing, strawberries ripe, and the very first cherries. It's hard to believe it's only the middle of May. There

are no gooseberries in Italy — and I like
them so much.

Mirenda. 11 June, 1927.

I keep hearing about "David".
Apparently the show was really quite a
success — people talk a good deal about
it. The critics don't matter — they are
too stale and false.... I am feeling better
since the summer is here and one lounges
about all day. We get up at six and sleep
a bit in the afternoon. It's very quiet and
nice.... I am writing my essays about the
Etruscans, that I've talked about so much,
and never got done — Let's hope I have
luck with them this time — and painting
a smallish picture — " Finding of Moses "
— all negresses. It's amazing, because I

159

don't quite know how to do it.... One is
never quite easy in one's mind these days....
I'm nearly forty-two. Talk about making
old bones, we're getting on.

To Miss Cooper.

Mirenda, 21 June, 1927.

.... I heard from Emily from Yarmouth,
but Ada didn't write. I think they all had
a good time. It's a pity they didn't have
some of the hot weather from here. We've
got it really fierce, except that there is a
little cool wind from the mountains. I've
never known the sun so strong for the time
of the year. We too were away at the
seaside about a hundred miles from here,
not far, a place called Forte dei Marmi.
Maria Huxley motored us down.... But I

am not fond of the flat sandy shores in
Italy. The sea is so dead and lifeless and
enervating. The rocky shore is best on the
Mediterranean. It isn't eight o'clock in the
morning, but the sun is already fierce, and
the cicalas — big grasshoppers — are
singing away in the trees, till you'd think
a dozen little people were working little
sewing-machines outside. The flowers are
over — cherries and strawberries finished
— the apricots just coming. Everywhere
the peasants are cutting the wheat. It's a
fine crop this year, tall and handsome, and
a lovely purply brown colour. All the
family set out at about four in the morning,
and they work one behind the other, women
and men and girls, cutting away with the
sickles, and laying the armfulls by: just as
Ruth did in the Bible. Then they leave off

161

about eleven, and eat, then sleep till four or five in the afternoon, then work again till eight or half past, when the fireflies are drifting about. But when the corn is cut the fireflies go.

Sometimes I think it would be good to be healthy and limited like the peasants. But then it seems to me they have so little in their lives, one had better just put up with one's own bad health, and have one's own experiences. At least they are more vivid than anything these peasants know.

Paris (undated).

I still don't hear anything from Seltzer, so shall probably come to London on Tuesday. Were at Versailles yesterday —

a silly big place — and bitter cold. But sunny today.

Still only a postcard — but I'll write a letter in a day or two, and send a photograph that Emily asked for, — one of each sort I'll send. I shall be leaving here on Saturday or Monday at latest — to go to Florence for just a day or two — C/O. G. Orioli, 6 Lungarno Corsini. — I was tempted to come to England — but the long journey — then the things they say about the pictures put me off terribly. You'll have to come and see me. I wonder if Frieda is coming to see you this week — I expect so. If she doesn't want to go to Germany I suppose we'll meet in Milan on the 11th or 12th — have written her to the Kingsley. Luckily it's not too hot here — but it may be any day — so I'm prepared to leave. Expect you have got a copy of the Pansies - I have.

Villach.

Karuten, Austria.

8 Aug. 1927.

It's so nice to be out of that hot Italy, and in the mountains where the air is cool. I can imagine nothing better than a really cool bed after one that burned when you lay in it, and really fresh mountain water after that tepid Italian stuff. Of course it was a specially hot summer, even for Tuscany — and quite exceptionally dry, no rain for three months. I wouldn't have minded if I'd been well, but being seedy, how I hated it.

I feel much better already here, and can take little walks into the country. This is a small old-fashioned town, with a nice full swift river, the Drave, and trees along the river, and seats where one can sit and watch the people and the swallows, and feel like an old veteran. There are lots of summer visitors passing all the time to the lakes and mountains — practically all Viennese. They wear any kind of clothes — the men the short Tyrolese leather trousers and bare legs. They are big strapping people — rather vague now — gone indifferent to all the woes. The country itself is dirt-poor — the shops are pathetic — all the rubbishy stuff nobody else will buy. Nearly all the banks closed for good — and the ordinary people having very little money. But they don't seem to care. They aren't very honest, they don't

give you your change — that kind of thing:
but even that they do so vaguely, they don't
really care.   There is no sense of control
at all — most queer, after the bossiness of
Fascist Italy.   And the whole thing drifts
along with no trouble, everybody really
very nice, very good-mannered — pleasant.
It's a great rest after Italy, and I hope I
shall soon feel fit for long walks. I can only
go small ways yet —.   We shall stay on in
this inn in town, I think, it is so amusing,
and one can go excursions.

Villach.   Austria.

27 Aug. 1927.

I am a good bit better now — cough
still a nuisance, but less than it was.
Yesterday it poured with rain, and at
evening the mountains came out white with

snow, almost to the foot — and the air is almost freezing. It is still icy cold this morning, but the sun is out, so it won't last.

I do get sick of these discontented women, who'd be discontented if you gave them Paradise in their hand.... What are things like among the miners? — are they rather depressed? The foreign papers give a bad account of the condition of England — trade and so on. But one never knows.

We came here on Wed. evening — met Else in Munich — it is just the same, the little wooden house in a corner of the forest, so still and pleasant. I like it here, and really feel much better. I had your letter, and so glad G. * is so well — what a relief to think of her really going about comfortably. Autumn here, but lovely.

Nr. Munich
7 Sept., 1927.

I've been here a week now — it's awfully nice, the little wooden house and the forest behind, the big open country in front with the mountains. The weather is lovely, sunny all day, and the moon at night. I feel it suits me here. I drink goat's milk, and we walk through the woods — all beech and fir trees. There are lots of

* Miss Gertrude Cooper.

deer in winter and spring, but at this
season they draw away to the more remote
places. We've got a good servant: the one
we knew in the past....

Germany is much more cheerful than
Austria — much more flourishing. In fact it
seems tremendously alive and busy. Austria
was too poor — too helpless, one couldn't
stand it long.... There's a new law that
takes 20% tax on all royalties of persons
living abroad — it came into force in July
last — so there's a slice off one's not very
grand earnings. But we're lucky to have
got off taxes so long.

Thumersbach. Germany (undated).

This is the villa — and our boathouse.
It has been hot also here — so we bathe

169

twice a day. We have four boats — must
row across to Zell for everything. Drove
yesterday with the pony to Ferlistur under
the glacier — very beautiful, the great
sloping white mass. The flowers a bit
higher up are really lovely. When do you
go to Llandudno? Hope you are having
a good time.

Germany. (undated).

Had your letter — you mustn't refuse
what I sent. We are leaving Monday —
I must go to Paris for a bit — business —
And Frieda will go to Baden. But Rhys
Davies will be coming along with me so I
shan't be alone. He was here this week, and
yesterday we drove in the carriage to le
Beausset and le Castelet — a lovely day —

pity you weren't there — but the country
still absolutely bare with frost, only a few
almond trees in blossom. Shall send address
in Paris — hope all goes well.

Mirenda, 19 Dec., 1927.

— says the miners are only working two
or three days a week. What do they say
to it? What do the young fellows say? I
should like to know how they take it.

To his nephew. Jack Clarke.

Florence

28 Dec. 1927.

Very many thanks for the pup — so you
snipped him out all by yourself! Which is
more than I'd know how to do. And such

171

neat genteel handwriting! My dear Jack, I hope you're not getting too good to be true. We had quite a nice Christmas — seventeen peasants in to the tree, all very happy singing. Christmas day we were in Florence — the Huxleys motored us in to friends in a villa there — and we had another tree. Your mother hasn't written at all but I suppose she had my letter. What did you do with your ten bob?

Mirenda. Florence.

6 January 1928.

— The peasants came in on Christmas Eve — seventeen of them. We have a lovely big pine tree that Pietro stole in the wood, ten feet or more tall, but the bits of

172

Christmas things on it look very small. It is dense and green, and when the candles are lit, suggests a forest — very nice. The peasants sang to us, and were happy.... I think we shall definitely give up this place in Spring, it's not a good climate, always changing. Perhaps we may go to the ranch, just for the summer, if I can afford it: and try to sell it. I know we should never *live* there. Then really I'd try Devonshire or somewhere there for a time, and if it suits me, really make a home there. I feel I'd like a permanent place somewhere, one gets older, and my health really has been a nuisance. It would be better to settle down if one could but find a place. Anyhow the year has turned. 1927 was a bad one, let's hope this will be better for us all. How are the pits working?

To Miss Cooper.

.... I'm a lot better. It's the vilest weather — been bitter cold, and this morning was trying to snow — but had to turn into cold rain, which has lasted all day. Poor Italy! The peasants have already lost the first crop of peas, and the broad beans — frozen about a month ago. The second crop of peas is in flower, so of course they're trembling, for fear they shall be frozen too. But I don't think they will — I think it is going to turn warmer.

The country looks very brown and bleak — had no rain for months, till a fortnight ago. But the flowers are all out — the field dark with sweet violets — and grape hyacinths everywhere — and the scarlet

174

and purple anemones, and the red tulips
out in the young wheat. Yet somehow the
flowers look lonely and a bit forlorn this
year — the grass is not revived yet, brown,
and everything brownish except the wheat....
What a mercy if you can but get brisk and
alert again. But you'll see you will. The
wheel is coming round to our side again.

Palma de Mallorca, Spain.
24 March, 1928. Thursday.

Had your letter — how nice the
greenhouse sounds! Hope you heard
nothing of the silly rumour that I am ill —
I'm perfectly all right. We think of taking
the ship to Marseilles on June 4th. and
going on to Italy — Frieda is so keen on
finding a house before the hot weather

starts, so we shall have to move soon. I think perhaps Italy is best to *live* in. I've had proofs of all my pictures except one, so the book is nearly ready — promised for June 1st. — and the show ought to open about the same time, though I've had no definite date yet. The book will be rather fine — you can either pick up your copy in London or I'll have it sent. Weather lovely and cool.

Florence, 1928.

No, I'm not any worse — but my bronchials are a bit tiresome, as ever. But I'm better on the whole. — I'll order some more of those capsules now, the other things were only throat pastilles and cough drops — which I take if I need them. We want to leave for Switzerland in about a fortnight.

176

But don't you go worrying about me — I'm fatter and all right except for that asthmatic cough, my old friend — and I can do anything except climb hills.

Florence, 1928.

Had your letter — afraid the hanky has gone into an Italian pocket, and tie round an Italian neck. Now Emily sent a quarter of tea by letter — it also does not arrive. No good! It has been such damp weather we have decided to go to Diablerets to join the Huxleys — in the snow about 4,000 ft. over lake Geneva, Switzerland. We leave next Monday. I'll write from there and send an address. Everybody says it is the best thing for me, so one can but try. I dread it rather. Hope you're all well.

Chalet Beau Site
Les Diablerets (Vand) 1928.

Here we, are, really in the snow — had
quite a good journey from Florence —
came tinkling along here in a sledge. There
are about 100 people in the hotel — winter
sporting — we have a flat in this chalet;
like a ship, all wood and low ceilings. It
isn't really cold, because there's no wind,
and the snow is dry. I think it'll suit me,
really.

Kesselmatte (Bern),
Switzerland. 1928.

We have been very bold — taken a little
peasant chalet away up on the mountain,
4,000 ft. — we two alone. The peasants
have moved across to their hay hut across

the valley. We only came this afternoon
— now its the first evening, and feels
queer.... When do you go to the sea?

Kesselmatte.
(Bern) Switzerland.
16 Aug., 1928.

Today it feels like Autumn and the
turning of the year. The peasants bring us
bilberries, and soon it will be cranberries.
We drove over the pass the other day to
Diablerets.   It looked so different in
summer, you wouldn't know it was the
same place. But a lot of not very pleasant
tourists — I really preferred it in winter.
In summer it's nicer on this side. The —s
had friends at the hotel — and Mukerdji,
a Hindu writer who lives in America. He
was quite amusing — but Hindus seem a
bit false to me over here.

I'm pretty well in myself, but my cough is a nuisance, as ever, and I simply cannot climb these slopes. I suppose I shall just have to put up with it and leave them unclimbed. Anyhow I don't care so much any more about walking and going to see places. Is Jack doing the fancy swimming and diving in the Mablethorpe pool? Just let me know when he breaks a record. As for Bertram, he's taking life pleasantly, I know: no thorns on his rose.

Switzerland, 10 Sept. 1928.

My God — these mincing young females all mincing together in a female bunch, they little know what a terrible thing they're preparing for themselves later, when this mincing young female business wears itself out. Are *all* young Englishwomen instinctively homosexual? Looks like it, to me. Of course I'm only speaking of the instincts, not of any practice. But that instinct sends a man's feelings recoiling to the ultimate pole. My God! what a ghastly mess " purity " is leading to! Poor Bertie, I sympathise with him — a prisoner already. I think it is quite wrong for young children to have so many hours schooling. Three hours in the morning would be *quite* enough, up to the age of eight. But I suppose one has to do as the world does, else be exceptional. As for myself I take my stand on exception.... We leave on the 17th for Baden Baden.... I don't think I shall come to England. The thought of it depresses me. Frieda will come to England for ten days or a fortnight. I want her to

see my picture show. Dorothy Warren opens
it either on the 5th or the 9th of Oct. The
first two days will be by invitation only.
I can have her send you a card if you wish
— but I'd advise you *not* to go — you won't
like the things. Best leave 'em alone. —
But the show will be open to the public till
the end of October.... The cows have now
all come down from the high Alps —
summer is over — time to go.

To his nephew. Jack Clarke.

Florence. 13 Sept. 1928.

I had your mother's letter just now, and
your " Riddings " snapshot. What a little
ruffian you are getting. I know we shall
have another scamp in the family. Great
news about the house — I must look round

for things for it. Ask your mother to tell me what kind of things she wants for it. With my love — so hot here still, and never any rain.

Florence, 1928.

We think to leave here on Sunday, for the French Alps near Grenoble. The Brewsters are in Florence and will go with us. Very muggy thundery weather here — it will be nice to get a bit higher up. We shall look round for a place about 3000 ft. and I shall write you as soon as we have an address. Nearly your birthday too.

Le Levandon. 1928.

Nice down here by the sea not far from Toulon. The others have all left — Else and the Huxleys — but am expecting Arabella and Richard Aldington — and Frieda next week. We may go over to the Island of Port Cros, so I'll send address in a day or two, when I'm sure. Am feeling very well.

La Vigie, Ile de Port Cros, Var.

France. 1928.

.... Its quite good fun here — an old fortified place on the top of the highest hill of the Island, but not a castle at all. Just an enclosed space, all gone wild, and smallish rooms on the inside, and outside a dry moat. Richard and Arabella are very nice — so is Brigit Patmore, a woman about my age whom we knew in the old

184

days. They are all busy doing literary work
— and they go off to swim. But it's an
hour's climb up from the sea, so with my
cold I don't go — we look down on the
green Island, all umbrella pines, and the
blue sea and the other isles, and the
mainland ten miles off. It's quite nice —
somehow doesn't move me very much....
And how are the miners working, now
winter is near again? I do hope it will be
a good friendly winter all round, not a
poisonous one.

Port Cros. 1928.

Well, the weather has bust up with a
vengeance — such gales, such torrents, no
boat able to come, no bread, and the poor

old vigie none too watertight. So we are all packing up and leaving — either next Tuesday or Thursday — as the sea allows us. I expect F. and I will just cross to the mainland and stay on the coast awhile — I'll let you know. I had your letter and the photographs — very swanky the new camera! Hope G. is keeping well.

Bandol, Var. 19 Dec. 1928.

.... a man Stephenson was here for two days — an Australian who publishes expensive books in London.... He says that after Christmas he will publish a book of reproductions of my paintings — a large sized book, to charge ten guineas a copy, seems to me a bit absurd, but there's this collecting craze nowadays.

.... I want to go to Spain.... I really feel
Italy isn't good for me just now — and here
is — and Spain would be. Somehow here
there isn't enough *to it* to make one want
to live — the country is a bit no-how, and
the French mess up their sea-side coast
worse than anybody — fearful hotch-potch
of villas, almost as bad as a slum.

Bandol, 11 Jan. 1929.

.... The beastly selfish self-consciousness
of the young makes them no fun to have
around.... You say you think I've hidden
some part of myself from you. Not at all.
I am always the same. But there is
something you just refuse to see and refuse

187

to accept in me. You insisted on a certain idealisation, and there it was! It's just the same thing makes you thankful — isn't going to read " Lady C. " Little — like — at her age, ought to be made to read " Lady C. " aloud and in company — make them get over some of their priggishness and self-conceit. All this hush-hush stuff is just filthy. Do you suppose people don't *have* any private thoughts? Of course they do. Much better the thing should be open.

Amalfi, 27 Jan. 1929.

We have come a trip to the mainland tired of the post strike and the railway strike and no letters and no work possible. Amalfi is marvellous — the picture shows the cloisters of this hotel where we are —

it was an old monastery. It is blazing sun, so hot we are sunburned — we came eight miles by steamer, eight miles on foot, and twelve miles in carriage. The coast is full of flowers — crocuses, violets, narcissi, and purple anemones, wild everywhere — and peach and almond in full flower — and beans and peas in flower and potatoes being dug — I do wish you were here. The strike has ended today.

Paris, (with Huxleys)
Spring 1929.

.... One feels so scattered and a bit bewildered in these towns — so much talk and fuss and nothing very real.... Secker is going ahead to do an expurgated edition of the " Pansies " — leave out a few poems.

Stephenson sent me the reproduction of another of my pictures — also very dim and vague and disappointing. I am sad about them. But of course other people don't know them as I do. — Paris at the moment is very sunny and warm, but there's not a flower anywhere, except in the shops — in all the Bois — like Hyde Park — not a spark of anything — a very dreary spring.

Mirenda - 1 April 1929.

.... I painted six or seven water-colours, sort of series. I might show them with my big pictures in a gallery in Bond St. some time this summer. How folks will dislike them!

Did I tell you Martin Secker is going to publish my collected poems in two vols. I

don't know exactly when, but I've corrected
the proofs. And he's got a vol. of short
stories ready. Various things all at once!
But I don't think I'm any more popular than
I was. Not my destiny to be popular.

There are lots of flowers in their own
places — but the country still looks a bit
blasted. But suddenly the pear-blossom is
all out — almond and peach are over. If
only it wouldn't rain, and would be sunny!

To his nephew. Jack Clarke.
> Hotel Royal,
> Palma de Mallorca,
> > Spain, 1929.

Well here we are on an Island again —
Majorca this time. It reminds me of Sicily,
warm and brilliant in the sun — but it's

not so beautiful. I think we shall stay awhile
— perhaps all summer. Already met some
friends here — going to see them this
afternoon. How do you like this peasant's
house? *

Palma de Mallorca, Spain.

2 June, 1929.

.... Sorry you were worried — these fool
newspapers! I always say they are pining to
announce one's death. But they're too
" previous " .... Your garden must be quite
a triumph. Lilac was passing when we came
here two months ago. They are cutting the
corn — it is very dry, and will soon look like
autumn. And with you everything is just
coming to luxuriance. I think when we *do*

---

* A reference to the picture on the post-card.

settle down to a house, gardening will be my hobby too. But here the earth is as dry as dry rock.... I have corrected proofs for Martin Secker — he has omitted about a dozen poems, with my consent — no use raising a fuss — and he expects to get the book out this month. I will see he sends you a copy. But probably I shall get a small private edition issued, complete and unexpurgated, so that the poems appear just as they were written.... No definite news yet about the pictures — nor the book of them. I have got proofs of all except one — so I shouldn't be surprised if Stephenson suddenly issues the book this week or next. You see, since the great scare of Jix and suppression, all publishers are terrified of the police — lest they come in and confiscate the whole edition. That would be a terrible loss in the case of my book of pictures, as it has cost about £ 2,000 to produce. But already there are orders for more than half — and the ten copies in vellum at fifty guineas each were ordered six times over. Madness!

Florence, 10 July, 1929.

.... Yes, one feels very sick about the pictures — I suppose they won't let them burn them.... Well, it's an unpleasant world — but I shan't let it worry me more than it need — and don't you either. The dirty swine would like to think they made you weep.

Baden Baden. 19 July 1929.

Pretty hot here too, but not like Italy — the others want to go up higher next week — not far from here — about 3,000 ft. — No further news from London.

194

Kurhäus Plattig - bei Bühl

(Baden)

28 July, 1929.

Had your letter and snaps yesterday —
I suppose it will be cooler now — here it
has thundered and rained so much it is really
cold, and we hug ourselves inside our
overcoats. We are in this hotel about
2,600 ft. up — Frieda and her mother and
I — and I think we shall stay about another
week — then go down to Baden and perhaps
on to Bavaria. I must say I don't like the
north — something depressing about it —
long for olive trees and the sight of the
Mediterranean. But I suppose this is good
for one. How nice, your garden! And soon
you'll be off to the sea!

2 Aug., 1929.

'Glad Jack is becoming such a prize lad at school! — Not that I think much of schools and their prizes.

Baden-Baden. 12 Aug. 1929.

.... How well I remember that cold Flamborough, which I loved, and Robin Hood's Bay, which I thought so beautiful!... I have been to the doctor too, the one who examined me two years ago. He says my lung is much better, much healed up, and the bronchial condition better, but still bad — and asthma bad. He now says not to go to altitudes — before he said up to 3,000 ft. Now he says the sea — and I know that's best — the Mediterranean, that is — not those cold seas.

We had telegrams from Dorothy (Warren)

and from the lawyer, but so far, not a single
letter about the case. It seems curious. I
have seen two English newspapers —
disgusting, how one is insulted! I shall
not forgive it easily, to my white-livered lot!
Thank God I needn't live among them, even
to hear their beastly mingy British voices.
Of course it makes us both very angry....
a lot of rats with long tails! However the
best will be to forget it as soon as possible.
No, I don't want to sell them (the pictures).

Baden Baden. Sunday.

August 1929.

(*Lawrence had visited the Kurhaus and
the Marionette Theatre — which he
described as* " very pretty and elegant ").
.... It was a lovely day — the beech trees
just going yellow, and a soft blue sky and

197

clear sun, the rather elegant park, and the woods beyond, on the steep hills — but it all belongs to sixty years ago, to the days of Turgenev and King Edward and heaps of money flowing. The Kurhaus — where the concerts and gambling and all that took place, is much more elegant and lovely than Monte Carlo. But the modern public is a dreary thing.

Well, I hope things are shaping all right now. Coal in England is done, and the colliers are done in, poor devils! It makes one sick. But it's the end of an epoch. God knows what comes next.

Rottach.

Bavaria.

28 Aug. 1929.

Very nice here, so sunny and still — I like it much better than Baden — and we have friends here.

Rottach. 1929.

We are leaving here next Tuesday, and going to S. of France — probably Bandol again for the winter.

Villa Beau Soleil, Bandol, Var.
17 Oct., 1929.

.... Had a bad cold and been in bed, but getting up a bit tomorrow. I somehow went all wrong in Germany, in my health — and this little bout is the result. But it is also a getting straight again. I shall be better after....

We've been in our little house two weeks now and like it. It's right on the sea — I lie and watch the sea and the islands, so

199

lovely, this blue, still autumn weather, like
a dream.... If we really like it here for
this winter, we shall get a house for a
permanency — this or another.... When
there is an opportunity I shall send you a
copy of " The Escaped Cock ", which rich
friends have just brought out in Paris —
500 copies, but all going to New York.
It is very beautifully done — I don't want
it to go to England at all. Did you see the
Risen Lord in last week's " Everyman "? —
or the week before. They asked me for an
article, but I was surprised they printed it.

I want my health to get better now — and
I feel it will. Germany was curiously bad
for me — so was Paris last spring. The fact
of the matter is, I shouldn't come north.
It always makes me ill. We'd better get a
permanent place somewhere down here.

Bandol, Var., 10 Dec. 1929.

.... My health is rather a nuisance — doesn't recover very well from the set-back in the summer. But I hope the turn of the year will improve it. Walking is the worst — I hardly go a stride — much worse than last year. Yet in myself I don't think I'm worse. But what a weariness it is!... We've had a few lovely sunny days, but really rather too warm. The yellow narcissus are in full flower — and the fresh young radishes and new potatoes are very good — grown since the rain.... That " Obscenity " pamphlet has already sold over 6,000 — quite a stir.

Bandol. Var. (undated).

.... I felt awfully unhappy after you had left this afternoon — chiefly because you

201

seem miserable, and I don't know what to say or do. But don't be miserable — or if you must be, at least realise that it's because of a change that is happening inside us, a change in feeling, a whole change in what we find worth while and not worth while. The things that seemed to make up one's life die into insignificance, and the whole state is wretched. I've been through it these last three years — and suffered, I tell you. But now I feel I'm coming through, to some other kind of happiness. It's a different kind of happiness we've got to come through to — but while the old sort is dying, and nothing new has appeared, it's really torture. But be patient, and realise it's a process that has to be gone through — and it's taken me three years to get even so far. But we shall come through, and be really peaceful and happy and in touch. You will see, the future will bring big changes — and I hope one day we may all live in touch with one another, away from business and all that sort of world, and really have a *new* sort of happiness together. You'll see — it will come — gradually — and before not so very many years. This is the slow winding up of an old way of life. Patience — and we'll begin another, somewhere in the sun.

Beau Soleil - Bandol.

15 January 1930.

.... My health has been rather better.

Beau Soleil, Bandol.

(undated).

.... You mustn't mind if it's a long time between letters — nowadays I find it simply an effort to write — in fact, I don't really do anything, writing or painting or anything else — unusual for me, but I suppose it's a mood. My health is better, but not very good — and I simply don't want to do anything on earth, even read.... Many people seem angry over my obscenity pamphlet, but Charlie Lake said he had sold three dozen and only three copies of Jix's. People need something to scrap about.

Beau Soleil - Bandol.

3 Feb., 1930.

.... I have decided to go to the Sanatorium that Dr. Morland recommended — Ad Astra, Vence A.M.... It is above Nice, I've arranged to go on Thursday.... But you won't want to come here when I'm in Vence, and they will

let me have visitors only twice a week. So
wait a bit, till I'm walking about, and then
come to Vence — they say it's nice there....
Of course I hate going — but perhaps it
won't be so bad.

Lawrence died in this Sanatorium on 2.nd
March 1930.

Vence, 1930.

I am about the same, anyhow no worse.
We are moving into a house here at Vence
on Saturday, and I'm having a nurse. —
I am telegraphing Warren to hold pictures
awhile, because the Aga Khan came with his
wife this afternoon and is so keen to show
them to artists in a private gallery in Paris.
He was very nice — so we'll see.

Ad Astra, Vence, 1930.

Got here yesterday — think I shall be all
right — quite nice and not alarming. Frieda
is in the hotel — I have a balcony and see
the coast-line and Cannes five miles off.
Shall go downstairs to lunch next week, all
being well.

This was written very shortly before
Lawrence died.

EARLY WORK

OF

D. H. LAWRENCE

TO LETTICE, MY SISTER.

The shorn moon trembling indistinct on her path,
Frail as a scar upon the pale blue sky
Draws towards the downward slope: some sickness hath
Worn her away to the quick, so she faintly faces
Along her foot-searched way, her sorrow-closed eye
Down the sky's steep stairs charting no track for her.

Some say they see, though I have never seen
The dead moon heaped within the young moon's arms
For surely the fragile fine young thing had been
Too heavily burdened to mount the heavens so.
My heart, disturbed in its dream slow-stepping, alarms
Me lest you, my sister, should go heaped with such
                                    [shadow of woe.

Since Death from the mother moon has pared close to
                                    [the quick
And cast us forth like shorn thin moons to travel
Our chartered way among the myriad thick

209

Strewn stars of pallid people, and through luminous litter
Of lives that sorrows like mischievous, strange mice chavel
To strew round our way, to diminish each full star's glitter.

Since Death has delivered naked and thin and white,
Since the month of childhood is over, and we start afresh,
Since the beloved, faded moon that set us alight
Is delivered from us, herself born again amid the moan
Of all us flesh, and we stand in our nakedness, nesh
And fearful to file forth now for the first time alone,

Let us seek to win her back unto us. The moon
That is dead, the mother-love like light that flowed
To stead her womb around us, beyond the swoon
Of death, commingles in God's mighty gloom
Whence issue unblemished the atoms which, soft bestowed
Settle upon us magnetic, so we wax and bloom.

For out in the waste, wild soul space that shall
Sing like a chorus some day
Still plies the love of our mother for us, straining our
[way
Wise, wonderful strands of winds that are laden with
[rare
Effluence from suffering folk-stuff which death has laid
[bare
On the air for our nourishment, who from these weave
[fair on fair.

210

THE FLY IN THE OINTMENT

(A Blot)

The short story which Lawrence named "A Fly in the Ointment" or "A Blot" is one of the earliest examples of his work which has not been published previously. Muriel is the girl of Hagg's Farm whom he named Miriam in "Sons and Lovers". He wrote an Eastwood address on the manuscript and it is probable that he wrote it when staying with Ada during a holiday from Croydon.

Muriel had sent me some mauve primroses, slightly weather-beaten, and some honeysuckle, twine threaded with grey-green rosettes, and some timid hazel catkins. They had arrived in a forlorn little cardboard box, just as I was rushing off to school.

" Stick 'em in water! " I said to Mrs. Williams, and I left the house. But those mauve primroses had set my tune for the day: I was dreamy and tender; school and the sounds of the boys were unreal, unsubstantial; beyond these were the realities of my poor winter — trodden primroses, and the pale hazel catkins that Muriel had sent me. Altogether the boys must have thought me a vacant fool; I regarded them as a punishment upon me.

I rejoiced exceedingly when night came, with the evening star, and the sky flushed dark blue, purple, over the golden pomegranates of the lamps. I was as glad as if I had been hurrying home to Muriel, as if she would open the door to me, would keep me a little while in the fireglow, with the splendid purple pall of the evening against the window, before she laughed and drew up her head proudly and flashed on the light over the tea-cups. But Eleanor, the girl, opened the door to me, and I poured out my tea in solitary state.

Mrs. Williams had set out my winter posy for me on the table, and I thought of all the beautiful things we had done, Muriel and I, at home in the Midlands, of all the beautiful ways she had looked at me, of all the beautiful things I had said to her — or had meant to say. I went on imagining beautiful things to say to her looking at me with her wonderful eyes, from among the fir boughs in the wood. Meanwhile I talked to my landlady about the neighbours.

Although I had much work to do, and although I laboured away at it, in the end there was nothing done. Then I felt very miserable, and sat still and sulked. At a quarter to eleven I said to myself:

"This will never do," and I took up my pen and wrote a letter to Muriel.

" It was not fair to send me those robins "
— we called the purple primroses ' robins ',
for no reason, unless that they bloomed in
winter — " they have bewitched me. Their
wicked, bleared little pinkish eyes follow
me about and I have to think of you and
home, instead of doing what I've got to do.
All the time while I was teaching I got mixed
up with you. ' If the interest on a certain
Muriel be —' that was arithmetic. And I've
read the miserable pieces of composition on
' Pancakes ' over and over, and never seen
them, thinking — ' the primrose flowers
because it is so sheltered under the plum-
trees. They are black plums, with very
gummy bark. She is fond of biting through
a piece of hard bright gum. Then her lips
get sticky' ".

I will not say at what time I finished

my letter. I can recall a sensation of being blind, dim, oblivious of everything, smiling to myself as I sealed the envelope; putting my books and papers in their places without the least knowledge of so doing, keeping the atmosphere of Strelley Mill close round me in my London lodging. I cannot remember turning off the electric light. The next thing of which I am conscious is pushing at the kitchen door.

The kitchen is at the back of the house. Outside in the dark was a little yard and a hand-breadth of garden backed up by the railway embankment. I had come down the passage from my room in the front of the house, and stood pushing at the kitchen door to get a glass for some water. Evidently the oilcloth had turned up a little, and the edge of the door was under it.

I woke up irritably, swore a little, pushed the door harder, and heard the oilcloth rip. Then I bent and put my hand through the small space of the door to flatten the oilcloth.

The kitchen was in darkness save for the red embers lying low in the stove. I started, but rather from sleepy curiosity than anything else. Perhaps I ought to say that I opened my eyes a little. Pressing himself flat into the corner between the stove and the wall was a fellow. I did not feel alarmed: I was away in the midlands still. So I stood looking in dull curiosity.

"Why?" I said quite mildly. I think this very mildness must have terrified him. Immediately he shrunk together, and began to dodge about between the table and stove, whining, snarling, with an incredibly mongrel sound:

"Don't yer touch me — don't yer come grabbin' at me — I'll hit yer between the eyes with this poker — I ain't done nothin' to you — don't yer touch me, yer bloody coward."

All the time he was writhing about in the space in which I had him trapped, between the table and stove. I was much too amazed to do anything but stare. Then my blood seemed to change its quality. It went cool and sharp with disgust. I was accustomed to displays of the kind in school, and I felt again the old misery of contempt and disgust. He dared not, I knew, strike, unless by trying to get hold of him I terrified him to the momentary madness of such a slum rat.

"Stop your row!" I said, standing still and leaving him his room. "Shut your miserable row. Do you want to waken the children? "

" Ah, but don't yer touch me, don't yer come no nearer! "

He had stopped writhing about, and was crouching at the defensive. The little frenzy too, had gone out of his voice.

" Put the poker down, you fool! "

I pointed to the corner of the stove, where the poker used to stand. I supplied him with the definite idea of placing the poker, in the corner, and, in his crazy witless state, he could not reject it. He did as I told him, but indefinitely, as if the action were second-hand. The poker, loosely dropped into the corner, slid to the ground with a clatter. I looked from it to him, feeling further contempt for the nerveless knave. Yet my own heart had begun to beat heavily. His own indefinite clumsiness,

222

and the jingle of the poker on the hearth, unnerved him still more. He crouched there abjectly.

I took a box of matches from the mantelpiece and lit the gas at the pendant that hung in the middle of the bare little room. Then I saw that he was a youth of nineteen or so, narrow at the temples, with thin, pinched-looking brows. He was not ugly, nor did he look ill-fed. But he evidently came of the lowest breed. His hair had been cut close to his skull, leaving a tussocky fringe over his forehead to provide him with a " topping ", and to show that it was no prison crop which had bared him.

" I wasn't doing no harm, " he whined, resentfully, with still an attempt at a threat in his tones. " I 'aven't done nuffin' to you,

you leave me alone. What harm have I done? "

" Shut up, " I said. " Do you want to wake the baby and fetch everybody down? Keep your mouth shut! "

I went to the door and listened. No one was disturbed. Then I closed the door, and quietly pulled down the wide-opened window which was letting in the cold night air. As I did so I shivered, noting how chill and dreary the mangle looked in the yard, with the moonlight on its frosty cover.

The fellow was standing abjectly in the same place. He had evidently been rickety as a child. I sat down in the rocking-chair.

" What did you come in here for? " I asked, curious.

" Well, " he retorted insolently " an' wouldn't you, if you 'adn't a place to go to of a night like this. "

" Look here, " I said coldly. " None of your sauce. "

" Well, I only come in for a warm " he said, meekly.

" Nor blarney either, " I replied. " You came to pinch something, it's no use saying you didn't. What should you have taken? " I asked, curiously. He looked back at me uneasily, then at his dirty hands, then at me again. He had brown eyes, in which low cunning floated like oil on the top of much misery.

" I might 'a took some boots " he said simply. For the moment he could not help speaking the truth.

" And what right have you to pinch boots from people who can't afford to buy any more? " I said.

" I ain't never done it before! This is the first time. "

" You miserable creep! " I said. He looked at me with a flash of rat-fury.

" Where do you live? " I asked.

" Exeter Road. "

" And do you do any work? "

" I couldn't never get a job — except I used to deliver laundry — "

" And they turned you off for stealing? "

He shifted and stirred uneasily in his chair. As he was so manifestly uncomfortable I did not press him.

" Who do you live with? "

" I live at 'ome. "

" What does your father do? "

But he sat stubborn and would not answer. I thought of the gangs of youths who stood at the corner of the mean streets near the school, there all day long, month after month, fooling with the laundry girls, and insulting the passers-by.

" But ", I said, " what's going to become of you? "

He hung his head again and fidgeted in his chair. Evidently what little thought he gave to the subject made him uncomfortable. He could not answer.

" Get a laundry girl to marry you, and live on her? " I asked, sarcastically.

He smiled sicklily, evidently even a little bit flattered. What was the good of talking to him.

" You'll loaf at the street corner till you go rotten, " I said.

He looked at me sullenly.

" Well, I can't get a job " he replied, with insolence. He was not hopeless, but like a man born without expectations, apathetic, looking to be provided for, sullenly allowing everything.

" But, " I said, " if a man is worthy of

his hire, the hire is worthy of a man — and I'm damned if you're one. "

He grinned at me with sly insolence.

" It beats me that any woman 'ud let you touch her, " I said.

And then he grinned slyly to himself, ducking his head to hide the joke. And I thought of the coloured primroses, and of Muriel's beautiful pensive face. Then of him with his dirty clothes and his nasty skin.

" Well, " I said, " You're beyond me. "

He gave me a narrow, leering look from his sore eyes.

" You don't know everything, " he said, in contempt.

I sat and wondered. And I knew I could not understand him, that I had no fellow feeling with him. He was something beyond me.

" Well, " I said, helplessly " You'd better go. But for God's sake steal in different streets. "

I rose, feeling he had beaten me. He could affect and alter me, I could not affect nor alter him. He shambled off down the path. I watched him skulk under the lamp-posts, afraid of the police. Then I shut the door.

In the silence of the sleeping house I stood quite still for some minutes, up against the impassable rock of this man, beyond which I could not get. Then I climbed the stairs. It was like a nightmare. I thought he was a blot, like a blot fallen on my soul, something black and heavy which I could not decipher.

As I hung up my coat I felt Muriel's fat letter in my pocket. It made me a trifle sick.

" No, " I said, with a flush of rage against her perfect serene purity. " I don't want to think of her. "

And I wound my watch up sullenly, feeling alone and wretched.

RACHEL ANNAND TAYLOR

(A lecture delivered in Croydon.)

" Mrs. Rachel Annand Taylor is not ripe yet to be gathered as fruit for lectures and papers. She is young, not more than thirty; she has been married and her husband has left her, she lives in Chelsea, visits Professor Gilbert Murray in Oxford, and says strange, ironic things of many literary people in a plaintive, peculiar fashion.

" This then is raw green fruit to offer you, to be received with suspicion, to be tasted charily and spat out without much revolving and tasting. It is impossible to appreciate the verse of a green fresh poet. He must be sun-dried by time and sunshine of favourable criticism, like muscatels and prunes: you must remove the crude sap of living, then the flavour of his eternal poetry comes out unobscured and unpolluted by what is temporal in him — is it not so?

" Mrs. Taylor is, however, personally, all that could be desired of a poetess: in appearance, purely Rossettian: slim, svelte, big beautiful bushes of reddish hair hanging over her eyes which peer from the warm shadow; delicate colouring, scarlet, small, shut mouth; a dark, plain dress with a big boss of a brooch in the bosom. a curious carven witch's brooch; then long, white, languorous hands of the correct, subtle radiance. All that a poetess should be.

" She is a Scotch-woman. Brought up lonelily as a child, she lived on the Bible,

on the 'Arabian Nights', and later, on
Malory's 'King Arthur'. Her upbringing
was not Calvinistic. Left to herself, she
developed as a choice romanticist. She lived
apart from life, and still she cherishes a
yew-darkened garden in the soul where
she can remain withdrawn, sublimating
experience into odours.

" This is her value, then: that to a world
almost satisfied with the excitement of
Realism's Reign of Terror, she hangs out
the flag of Romance, and sounds the music
of citterns and viols. She is mediaeval; she
is pagan and romantic as the old minstrels.
She belongs to the company of Aucassin and
Nicolette, and to no other.

" The first volume of poems was published
in 1904. Listen to the titles of the poems:
' Romances ', ' The Bride ', ' The Song of

Gold ', ' The Queen ', ' The Daughter of Herodias ', ' Arthurian Songs ', ' The Knights at Kingstead ', ' Devotional ', ' Flagellants ', ' An Early Christian ', ' Rosa Mundi ', ' An Art-lover to Christ ', ' Chant d'Amour ', ' Love's Fool to His Lady ', ' Saint Mary of the Flowers ', ' The Immortal Hour ', ' Reveries ', ' The Hostel of Sleep '.

" I will read you four of the love songs. Against the first, in the book Mrs. Taylor gave me, I found a dried lily of the valley, that the author had evidently overlooked. She would have dropped it in the fire, being an ironical romanticist. However, here is the poem, stained yellow with a lily: it is called ' Desire ".

" That is the first of the love songs. The second is called ' Surrender '. The

third, which is retrospective is ' Unrealised ',
and the fourth is ' Renunciation '. There is
the story of Mrs. Taylor's married life, that
those who run may read. Needless to say,
the poetess' heart was broken.

" ' There is nothing more tormenting, ' I
said to her, than to be loved overmuch. '

" ' Yes, one thing more tormenting, ' she
replied.

" ' And what's that? ' I asked her.

" ' To love, ' she said, very quietly.

" However, it is rather useful to a poetess
or poet to have a broken heart. Then the
rare fine liquor from the fragile vial is
spilled in little splashes of verse, most
interesting to the reader, most consoling
to the writer. A broken heart does give
colour to life.

" Mrs Taylor, in her second volume, ' Rose

and Vine ', published last year, makes the splashes of verse from her spilled treasure of love. But they are not crude, startling, bloody drops. They are vermeil and gold and beryl green. Mrs Taylor takes the pageant of her bleeding heart, first marches ironically by the brutal daylight, then lovingly she draws it away into her magic, obscure place apart where she breathes spells upon it, filters upon it delicate lights, tricks it with dreams and fancy, and then re-issues the pageant.

" ' Rose and Vine ' is much superior to the Poems of 1904. It is gorgeous, sumptuous. All the full, luscious buds of promise are fullblown here, till heavy, crimson petals seem to brush one's lips in passing, and in front, white blooms seem leaning to meet one's breast. There is a great deal of sensuous colour, but it is all abstract, impersonal in feeling, not the least sensual. One tires of it in the same way that one tires of some of Strauss' music — ' Electra, ' for instance. It is emotionally insufficient, though splendid in craftsmanship.

" Mrs. Taylor is, indeed, an exquisite craftsman of verse. Moreover, in her metres and rhythms she is orthodox. She allows herself none of the modern looseness, but retains the same stanza form to the end of a lyric. I should like more time to criticise the form of this verse.

" However, to turn to ' Rose and Vine '. There is not much recognisable biography here. Most of the verses are transformed from the experience beyond recognition. A really new note is the note of motherhood. I often wonder why, when a woman artist comes, she never reveals the meaning of maternity, but either paints horses, or Venuses or sweet children, as we see them in the Tate Gallery, or deals with courtship, and affairs, like Charlotte Bronte and George Eliot. Mrs Taylor has a touch of the mother note. I read you ' Four Crimson Violets ' and now ' A Song of Fruition ' (' An October Mother '). What my mother would have said to that when she had me, an Autumn baby, I don't know!

" A fine piece of thoughtful writing is ' Music of Resurrection, ' which, significantly opens the ' Rose and Vine ' volume.

" That was last year. This year came the ' Hours of Fiametta ' — a sonnet sequence. There are 61 sonnets in the Shakespeare form, and besides these, a ' Prologue of Dreaming Women, ' an ' Epilogue of

Dreaming Women ' and an Introduction. In the Introduction Mrs Taylor says there are two traditions of women — the Madonna, and the dreaming woman.

" The latter is always, the former never, the artist: which explains, I suppose why women artists do not sing maternity. Mrs Taylor represents the dreaming woman of today — and she is almost unique in her position, when all the women who are not exclusively mothers are suffragists or reformers.

" Unfortunately, Mrs Taylor has begun to dream of her past life and of herself, very absorbedly; and to tell her dreams in symbols which are not always illuminating. She is esoteric. Her symbols do not show what they stand for of themselves: they are cousins of that Celtic and French form of symbolism which says — ' Let X = the winds of passion, and Y = the yearning of the soul for love. '

"' *Now the dim, white petalled Y*
Draws dimly over the pallid atmosphere
The scalded kisses of X. '

Mrs. Taylor has begun the same dodge.

"' *Since from the subtle silk of agony*
Our lamentable veils of flesh are spun. '

"' Subtle silk of agony ' may claim to sound well, but to me it is meaningless.

" But I read you the ' Prologue of Dreaming Women, " which surely is haunting: —

" How dare a woman, a woman, sister of Suffragists and lady doctors, how dare she breathe such a thing! But Mrs Taylor is bolder still. Listen to the ' Epilogue of Dreaming Women. " It is, I think, a very significant poem, to think over and to think of again when one reads ' Mrs. Bull. '

" But these are not Fiammetta. They are her creed. Her idiosyncracies are in the sonnets, which, upon close acquaintance, are as interesting, more interesting far to trace than a psychological novel. I read you only one, No. 18. Some of these sonnets are very fine: they stand apart in an age of ' open road ' and Empire thumping verse. "

ART AND THE INDIVIDUAL

The following paper on " Art and the Individual " was probably delivered in Croydon. It appears that it was written for members of a study circle, but Lawrence made no reference to this in letters to his sister.

" These Thursday night meetings are for discussing social problems with a view to advancing a more perfect social state and to our fitting ourselves to be perfect citizens — communists — what not. Is that it? I guess in time we shall become expert sociologists. If we would live a life above the common ruck we must be experts at something — must we not? Besides, we have peculiar qualities which adapt us for particular parts of the social machine. Some of us make good cranks, doubtless each of us would make a good hub of the universe. They have advanced the question

249

in education — 'Where in the school shall we begin to specialise?' Specialise, that's the word! This boy has a strong, supple wrist; let him practise pulling pegs out of a board like a Jap dentist's apprentice, then he'll be an expert tooth puller. Under Socialism every man with the spirit of a flea will become a specialist — with such advantages it were disgraceful not to cultivate that proverbial one talent, and thus become a shining light on some tiny spot. It will take some four hundred specialists to make a normal family of four. However!

" Now listen to the text which describes the ultimate goal of education. 'The ultimate goal of education is to produce an individual of high moral character. " Take that on the authority of the great expert. Moral character consists, I suppose, in a good sense of proportion, a knowledge of the relative effects of certain acts or influences, and desire to use that knowledge for the promoting of happiness. The desire you may easily possess. We are all altruists. But what about the knowledge, the sense of proportion? How can you have an idea of proportional values unless you have an extensive knowledge of or at least acquaintance with the great influences which result in action. Here is the immediate goal of education — and our real purpose of meeting here, after that of making ourselves heard, is to educate ourselves. The immediate goal of education is to gain a wide sympathy, in other words a *many-sided interest.*

" Let us look at Herbart's classification of interests, adding one that he overlooked.

	Knowledge Intellectual	1. Empirical.
		2. Speculative.
		3. Aesthetic.

Interest arising from

	Sympathy Emotional.	4. Sympathetic.
		5. Social.
		6. Religious.

Action.

EMPIRICAL:

Interest in concrete individual things (I see a swan — it sails up to me and attracts my attention. I notice how it shows itself off to me — it pecks under the water — it swims nearer — I observe its wings magnificently arched) — (evening flowers).

SPECULATIVE:

Interest in deeper connections and causes of events — scientific and philosophic interests (it is remarkable that the swan should raise its wings so proudly — why can it be — evening flowers).

AESTHETIC:

Interest aroused neither by phenomena nor causes as such, but by the approval which their harmony and adaptability to an end win from me. (The swan is very beautiful — the moon-light on the flowers is lovely — why does it move me so?)

SYMPATHETIC:

Social: Growing comprehension of the incorporation of the individual in the great social body whose interests are large beyond his personal feelings. He is a unit, working with others for a common welfare, like a cell in a complete body.

RELIGIOUS:

When this extended sympathy is directed to the history (origin) and destiny of mankind, when it reverentially recognises the vast scope of the laws of nature, and discovers something of intelligibility and consistent purpose working through the whole natural world and human consciousness, the religious interest is developed and the individual loses for a time the sense of his own and his day's importance, feels the wonder and terror of eternity with its incomprehensible purposes. This, I hold it, is still a most useful and fruitful state. Note parallelism of 1, 2, 3, — 4, 5, 6, — increasing height of planes.

" Which of these forms of interest are we most likely to neglect? Consider — the aesthetic is our present consideration. Since we have accepted the Herbartian broad interpretation, we must take a broad view of Art to fit it, since Aestheticism embraces all art. Examine the definition, ' The Approval which the Harmony and Adaptability to an end win from us. '

" It is vague and unsatisfactory. Look closely. ' Approval of Harmony ' — That is a pleasurable experience. We see or hear something that gives us pleasure — we call it harmony — invert it — we see or hear harmonious blendings — we feel pleasure. We are not much further, except that we recognise that the ultimate test of all harmony, beauty, whatever you call it, is in *personal feeling*. This would place aesthetic interest under the emotional group. Look at it again. ' Approval of adaptability of things to an end. ' Here is harmony again — but it is more comprehensible, more intellectual. We see a good purpose in sure and perhaps uninterrupted process of accomplishment. It is gratifying — we are glad — why? Because, I believe, we are ourselves almost unconscious agents in a great inscrutable purpose, and it gives us relief and pleasure to consciously recognise that power working out in things beyond and apart from us. But that is aside.

" There have been two schools of Aesthetic thought since the beginning of such thought.

(1) Art. Beauty is the expression of the perfect and divine Idea. This is the mystic Idea, held by Hegel, ' Beauty is the shining of the Idea through matter. '

(2) a. Art is an activity arising even in the animal kingdom and springing from sexual desire and propensity to play

(Darwin, Schiller, Spencer) and it is accompanied by pleasurable excitement.

b. Art is the external manifestation by lines, colour, words, sounds, movements of emotion felt by man.

c. Art is the production of some permanent object or passing action filled to convey pleasurable impression quite apart from personal advantage.

" In the interpretation we have accepted, these two, the mystical and the sensual ideas of Art are blended. Approval of Harmony — that is sensual — approval of Adaptation — that is mystic — of course none of this is rigid. Now apply the case to our swan.

I. Approval of Harmony (Beauty we will say) — there is the silken whiteness, the satisfying curve of line and mass. Why do these charm us? I cannot answer.

" Turn to Adaptation: - Now we might say that we love the silken whiteness and the grandly raised wings because they are the expression of the great purpose which lead the swan to raise itself as far as possible to attract a mate, the mate choosing the finest male that the species may be reproduced in its most advantageous form. That you must sift for yourselves. But there is a sense (perhaps unconscious) of exquisite harmony and adaptation to an end when we feel the boat-like build of the bird, the strength of those arched wings, the suppleness of the long neck which we have seen waving shadowily under the water in search of food. Contrast the quaint gobbling, diving ducks. Think too of our positive pain in seeing the great unwieldy body of the bird, standing on the bank supported by ugly black legs. Why is it ugly? Because a structure like that could *not* walk with ease or grace — it is unfitted to its surroundings. The legs are hateful because, being black, they are too violent a contrast to the body which is so white — they are clammy looking too — and what sense is ' clammy ' applied to? Think of evening primroses in the moonlight and in the noonday. Flowers and insects have evolved side by side.

" This is Beauty in Nature — but does the same hold good when we turn to the human productions of Art? Often it does. But think of the works of Poe, of Zola, de Maupassant, Maxim Gorky, Hood's ' Song of the Shirt ' — think of Watts' Mammon (if that is Art) of the Laocoon, the Outcasts of Luke Filde. Do you experience any

259

' pleasure ' in these? Do they excite
' pleasurable feelings? ' Do they show
Divine purpose? Yet they are Art. Why?
Somebody would say, ' They are so true. '
But they are not necessarily true, in the
strict sense of the word. Not true, except
that they have been felt, experienced as if
they were true. They express — as well
perhaps as is possible — the real *feelings*
of the artist. Something more then, must
be added to our idea of Art — it is the
medium through which men express their
deep, real feelings. By ordinary words,
common speech, we transmit thoughts,
judgments, one to another. But when we
express a true emotion, it is through the
medium of Art.

" When Carlyle said that a hero could
hardly express himself otherwise than

through song, he meant that the vigorous emotion so moulded the speech of his hero — Mahommet, Dante, Burns, — that this speech became Art. So Art is the second great means of communication between man and man, as Tolstoi says. Intellectual Art, which has no emotion, but only wit, has cold barren effect. Think of Pope and the great Encyclopedists. This means of communication of emotion is in three ways — by form and colour (as in all painting, sculpture, weaving, building) — by sound (music) by ideas through words — all literature down to the graphic, moving tale told by a boy to his mates. The picture words, the thrilling voice, the animated face and lively gestures, all go to make up the art of story-telling. The English, whatever is said of them, are a truly poetic people, if reserved. Look at our words — words like ' flash ', ' laughter ', ' wonder '. Compare Latin and French, ' rideo ' and ' rire '.

" The essence then of true human art is that it should convey the emotions of one man to his fellows. It is a form of sympathy, and sympathy is in some measure harmony and unity, and in harmony and unity there is the idea of consistent purpose, is there not? So it works back to the old definition. But, you will say, there are emotions desirable and undesirable — and Art may transmit the undesirable. Exactly — then it is bad Art. According to the feeling that originated it, Art may be bad, weak, good, in all shades. So Tolstoi says that all nude study is bad art — Honi soit qui mal y pense.

" This might lead you to reflect that anyone who feels deeply must be an artist. But there you must consider that not one person in a thousand can express his emotions. We are most of us dumb, there, or we can only talk to a few who understand our mute signs, and the peculiar meanings we give to the words we use. The same sentence in ten different mouths has ten different meanings. We can feel, but we cannot transmit our feelings — we can't express ourselves. When you have tried, when you have felt compelled to write to somebody, for you could not contain yourself, what sort of a letter has it appeared when written? Weak, maudlin, ridiculous — Why? You didn't feel ridiculous. But you did not understand what effect certain words have on readers.

You didn't find the picture word, you didn't use a quick, spirited, vigorous style, so your letter is *not* art, for it does *not* express anything adequately.

" This brings us to the technique of art. This again seems to be mostly a question of pleasurable feeling. Take these examples — of drawing — the physiological aspect — of music — of colour — the common basis. Now we are in a position to attempt criticism. Take Leighton's ' Wedded ' and Watts' ' Mammon '. We can excellently well criticise what we call the ' spirit ' of the thing — look! But we are not so well able to understand, or even to appreciate, the technique. That needs study. ' The chief triumph of art, ' says Hume, ' is to insensibly refine the temper and to point out to us those dispositions which we should

264

endeavour to attain by constant *bent* of mind and by repeated *habit.* '

" If we bend our minds, not so much to things beautiful, as to the beautiful aspect of things, then we gain this refinement of temper which can *feel* a beautiful thing. We are too gross — a crude emotion carries us away — we cannot feel the beauty of things. It is so in Socialism as in everything. You must train yourself to appreciate beauty or Art — refine yourself, or become refined, as Hume puts it. And what is refinement? It is really delicate sympathy. What then is the mission of Art? To bring us into sympathy with as many men, as many objects, as many phenomena as possible. To be in sympathy with things is to some extent to acquiesce in their purpose, to help on that purpose. We want, we are

265

for ever trying to unite ourselves with the whole universe, to carry out some ultimate purpose — evolution, we call one phase of the carrying out. The passion of human beings to be brought into sympathetic understanding of one another is stupendous; witness it in the eagerness with which biographies, novels, personal and subjective writings are read. Emotion tends to issue in action.

" In Socialism you have the effort to take what is general in the human character and build a social state to fit it. In Art is revealed the individual character. After all the part of a man's nature which is roughly common to all his fellows is only a small part of his nature. He must be more than that — more refined, to understand the host of the particular qualities which go to make up the human character and are influences in the progress of things. So, though art is general, it is also particular. Socialism is general.

" Think, we can still feel the arms of Ruth round the neck of Naomi, we can feel the tears in the womens' eyes. We too, can love and suffer at parting. We still count the story of David and Jonathan one of the finest in the world. There are other tales incomprehensible to us; and only a few can recognise the ideal, the noble emotion which many medieval artists espressed so perfectly in their Madonnas — moon faced Madonnas, we say, and turn aside. But with a little thought and study you might feel a sympathy grow up for these Madonnas, and understand. So through Art we may be brought to live many lives, taking a commonplace life as a unit, and each may have so many fields of life to wander in as never to feel wretched and empty. These things are not obvious and immediate, so we are apt to despise them. But above all things we must understand much if we would do much.

"In conclusion, I would like to suggest that whatever be the subject for discussion, everyone should try and make some study of it, think about it, and, if there is anything they feel inclined to say, say it. It would be a good idea, too, to take a book, socialistic essays, an essay of Mill or Spencer or anybody, something that costs little, and study it for full discussion one evening, someone presiding. We might at rare intervals, take a poet, painting, or a novel, or a play.

EARLY PAINTINGS

A VASE OF FLOWERS.

STILL LIFE.

THE STICK GATHERER.

AUTUMN.

TIGER'S HEAD.

" AN IDYLL " - (AFTER M. GREIFFENHAGEN).

LANDSCAPE.

LANDSCAPE - (AFTER COROT).

THE ORANGE MARKET (AFTER BRANGWYN).

A NOTE ON THE PROPER NAMES
IN THE NOTTINGHAMSHIRE NOVELS

In his Nottinghamshire stories Lawrence described places with which he had been familiar since childhood. Considerable confusion has been caused among readers owing to his habit of describing one part of the county and calling it by the name of another. In " The White Peacock " for instance he names Felley Mill, Strelley Mill. Strelley is a village which lies several miles away and the book has nothing to do with it. Nethermere is Moorgreen Reservoir. Highclose is Lamb Close the well known residence of the

271

owner of Brinsley Colliery where Lawrence's father was employed. He did not bother to change the name of the Ram Inn at Moorgreen and took the name of Mrs. May the neighbour who was so surprised by the " rots ", for the old woman of the inn which appears in " The White Peacock ". For Lettice Beardsall he took his sister Ada's first name and his mother's maiden name. Eberwich is Eastwood and so accurate are his descriptions that those who know the district are able to follow him almost step by step. The Kennels " famous in the time of Lord Byron " and the estate, are a description of the home of the Chaworth-Musters family at Annesley, and the woods are the beautiful High Park Woods. The old quarry in which the gamekeeper was killed is actually near Moorgreen Colliery.

Greymede Church is Greasley and the Abbey, Felley Abbey. In describing Sunny Bank be gave a picture of the Misk Hills. Tempest Warrall & Co. is meant to be Barber Walker & Co, a firm which largely developed the coal mining industry in Nottinghamshire.

In " The Lost Girl " he did not disguise characters who were known by everyone in Eastwood or " Woodhouse ". James Haughton was George Cullen, a remarkable man whose ideas of clothing were quite foreign to those of the miners and their wives. His shop, London House, named by Lawrence, Manchester House, was stocked with beautiful creations bought by him in London. He spent money on Throttle Ha Penny, the little pit at Hill Top, Eastwood and lost it, and opened a

cinema at Langley Mill, the Lumley of the
novel. His daughter became a nurse.
Although Lawrence drew so much on fact,
Alvina is his own creation. Knarborough
is Nottingham. He did not invent names
for Alfreton, Bulwell and Bagthorpe. The
Klondyke brickyard was at New Eastwood.

Cossethay of " The Rainbow " is Cossall
where Marsh Farm still lies near the canal
bank. Beldover is the village of Quorn in
Leicestershire. The cottage in which the
Brangwyns lived is near Cossall church.

In " The Virgin and the Gypsy " he varied
one or two names, Woodlinkin being
Wirksworth and Amberdale, Ambergate in
the Derbyshire hills. He lived at Mountain
Cottage at Middleton in Wirksworth for
some time during the war and became
familiar with the surrounding country.

The Bestwood of " Sons and Lovers " is Eastwood although there is a village and colliery named Bestwood not very far away. In this book he calls Barber Walker and Co. Carson Waite and Co. Selby is Brinsley Colliery. Nuttall is Underwood and has nothing to do with the picturesque village, now being rapidly spoilt by building speculators, which lies on the Nottingham-Eastwood main road. Minton is Moorgreen. Crich is Crich, one of the loveliest places in Derbyshire. Willey Farm is Hagg's Farm. He described the same part of the country in " The White Peacock. " There are no important alterations in " Aaron's Rod. "

In " Love Among The Haystacks " he returned to Greasley, describing the moving meadow opposite Greasley Church which he had already described in " The White Peacock. "